Phonetic Spelling
FOR COLLEGE STUDENTS

Phonetic Spelling

FOR COLLEGE STUDENTS

BY RALPH M. WILLIAMS

Trinity College, Hartford

GREENWOOD PRESS, PUBLISHERS
WESTPORT, CONNECTICUT

Library of Congress Cataloging in Publication Data

Williams, Ralph M
    Phonetic spelling for college students.

    Reprint of the ed. published by Oxford University
Press, New York.
    1. English language—Orthography and spelling.
2. English language—Phonetics. I. Title.
PE1143.W5 1980   421'.52   80-24084
ISBN 0-313-22650-4 (lib. bdg.)

© 1960 by Oxford University Press, Inc.

Reprinted with the permission of Oxford University Press, Inc.

Reprinted in 1980 by Greenwood Press
A division of Congressional Information Service, Inc.
88 Post Road West, Westport, Connecticut 06881

Printed in the United States of America

10 9 8 7 6 5 4 3 2 1

Preface

This book is the result of more than ten years of experimentation in a special class for weak spellers at Trinity College. I am most grateful to all the students who, willingly or otherwise, allowed me to experiment on them. Many of my ideas originally came from *Remedial Training for Children with Specific Disability in Reading, Spelling and Penmanship* by Anna Gillingham and Bessie W. Stillman (now in its fifth edition, this book may be obtained from Miss Gillingham at 25 Parkview Avenue, Bronxville 8, N.Y.). Miss Gillingham tells me that most of the work on spelling was done by the late Miss Stillman. The true significance of her work occurred to me while I was attending a course in structural linguistics offered at Trinity by Professor H. A. Gleason of the Hartford Seminary Foundation. Professor Gleason also read through and constructively criticized an early version of this book, so that I am doubly indebted to him. Later versions were read and helpfully commented upon by my colleague, Professor Walter D. Leavitt, and by Professor Dudley Bailey of the University of Nebraska. I wish to thank everyone at the Oxford University Press who has helped to prepare this book for publication. It should be clear, however, that with all this help it is obviously my fault if any flaws still remain in what follows.

R.M.W.

Hartford, Connecticut
June 1960

Contents

Phonetic Spelling
FOR COLLEGE STUDENTS

Introduction

One of the tragedies of being a poor speller is the result of the widespread conviction that not being able to spell is a sign of poor intelligence or laziness or both. The fact that this belief is widespread makes spelling assume a greater importance than it should, probably, especially when one is being judged by a letter of application, a social note, or some other example of one's spelling. But the fact that this belief is erroneous holds out some hope for the bad speller, and is the basic idea behind this little book.

This book is developed with the idea that most poor spellers are intelligent—intelligent enough to help themselves improve with proper guidance. This book is designed, therefore, for students *old enough and mature enough to want to help themselves,* for high school and college students primarily, but for older people too. The work is planned for a semester, or about fifteen weeks (depending on how many Review Lessons you do) of three lessons a week. You may be able to use this book as a "self-aid," working independently, but you will probably find it more satisfactory to have a teacher or older friend who will check your work to make sure that you are doing the exercises correctly.

It is not enough, we feel, to learn how to study words and to spell the words one has studied; life's varied situations are continually putting everyone in the position of having to spell unstudied words, and we wish to provide you with a method of dealing intelligently with those words. This means that you must concern yourself more with general rules or principles than with individual words and lists of words.

Strictly speaking, there are no "rules" of spelling, there are only phonetic generalizations—observations of the way the language usually represents sounds or handles specific spelling situations such as doubling final consonants. And English is far more consistent about such things than it is generally given credit for being. A majority of words in the language could possibly be spelled in only one way (i.e. each sound in the word is always represented by the same symbol), and so do not need to be studied at all by anyone who can hear and reproduce the sounds of the language and relate them to their symbols. This ability is the one thing we must take for granted in all our students if this book is to be of any help. You may find it necessary to get a little assistance from a roommate or friend with the exercises at the end of Chapter 1, in order to practice both the hearing and the speaking of the correct sounds. For a rare few who are physiologically unable to associate sound and symbol, this book will be worthless.

The remaining words in the language allow a choice of symbols for one or more of the sounds and hence are improperly called "unphonetic." Actually most of the choices are taken care of by phonetic generalizations which allow these words to be studied as groups. These generalizations, which constitute the majority of spelling generalizations, are the "meat" of this book. We do not, however, intend to overlook anything else which may be of help to the speller; we shall also discuss the spelling generalizations which are not limited to single sounds (though these are well presented in the section of your dictionary entitled "Orthography"), and we shall later tell you how to deal with the third and smallest group of words in the language, those that defy generalizations and do have to be studied individually.

Most good spellers use these generalizations subconsciously, even in tackling new words. The exercises in this book are designed to help you use them subconsciously too, though at first your work may seem very conscious. Not every generalization will apply to as many difficult words as some others; neither will every one be as generally true as the others. But using them, thinking about them as you write, and being on the alert to notice words to which a generalization applies, will all help to develop the right "frame of mind" for using these generalizations subconsciously.

If you like to play bridge, as I do, you will see here an analogy between learning to spell by generalizations and learning a new system of bidding. I am at the moment trying to learn how to bid by Goren's point-count method—evaluating my hand by counting aces as 4, kings as 3, queens, 2, jacks, 1. There are so many different things that one should do, depending on the total count in one's hand, that I still play with Goren's handbook on the table beside me, much as some poor spellers always write with their dictionaries on their knees. The difference is that I am learning generalizations from Goren's book, not individual "spellings." And as I use his generalizations and become familiar with them, I don't have to refer to the book so often; even though every new hand presents a new situation, the generalizations will cope with it. And so it is with this book; here are the generalizations—use them until you no longer need the book, even though every new word presents a new problem. We cannot promise to perform miracles, we cannot promise that you won't "get set" occasionally, but we sincerely believe that if you follow our suggestions as presented here, you can make yourself an improved and probably an acceptable speller.

The Sounds of English

Spelling is, for all practical purposes, a problem in writing. We may occasionally be asked by a friend how to spell a word, and have to spell it orally, but such occasions form so small a part of our total spelling of words that it is insignificant. Spelling, then, is the representation of spoken sounds by written symbols.

Now this is *not* going to be a book on linguistics, but we will find some of the terms and methods of the linguists very useful. One of these is their use of *minimal pairs,* that is, pairs of words such as *moon* and *noon,* or *bad* and *pad,* which differ in the smallest recognizable unit of sound possible. These different sounds, the smallest feature of the spoken language which differentiates what is said from what might have been said,[1] are called *phonemes.* This is a more accurate term than "sounds" because one phoneme is an absence of sound, the slight pause known as the "open transition" whose different position helps to distinguish *light housekeeper* from *lighthouse keeper.* Including this open transition, there are 35 phonemes in English with which we must be concerned in spelling.[2]

A trained linguist can differentiate several times as many sounds as these 35, and in the International Phonetic Alphabet has symbols for them all. No one language uses them all, but each may be found somewhere. And even in English, most speakers of the language use more than 35 different sounds in their speech. For example, the /g/ sounds in *geese* and *goose* are different, as are the /k/ sounds in *key* and *cool.* A native speaker of English has to be specially trained to hear the difference, because in English the difference creates no phonemic distinction, but speakers of Nootka, Kwakiutl, Bella Coola, and Eskimo would hear the difference at once, as the sounds do have phonemic value in their languages.[3]

And when we come to look at the dialects of English, we see an even greater variety of sounds used than ever occurs in the speech of any one individual. For example, the sound represented by *r* varies from the slight aspiration of some American dialects to the Scots /r/ with a trill or "burr" on it. Yet as these different sounds are not used to distinguish "what is said from what might have been said," they are not phonemes, but are what are known as *allophones.* The two varieties of /g/ mentioned in the preceding paragraph are allophones of the same phoneme, and those of /k/ are of another phoneme.

In other words, English spelling is an attempt to have one standard spelling represent many variant pronunciations of one word. It is more universal in this way than is speech, which is an advantage but one that brings disadvantages with it. It means, for example, that our generalizations will vary in usefulness from one dialect to another and from one generalization to another. It also means that we must consider more carefully just what

---

[1] H. A. Gleason, Jr., *An Introduction to Descriptive Linguistics,* New York, Henry Holt & Co., 1955, p. 9.

[2] The other eleven phonemes in English, the four levels of pitch, three clause terminals, and four levels of stress or accent, are more concerned with the sentence, and do not directly affect spelling. Word accent, although it influences sentence stress, is quite different, and it, of course, does affect spelling, as we shall see.

[3] Charles F. Hockett, *A Course in Modern Linguistics,* New York, Macmillan, 1958, p. 70.

is meant by the expression "phonetic spelling." Most people think of phonetic spelling as having one symbol for each sound (phoneme) and that symbol used only for that sound. But sometimes, as we shall note, both individual and dialectal variations in a word go even beyond the limits of allophones. What individual's set of sounds, or what dialect's set of sounds, is going to be used as the standard for the phonetic spelling? Obviously no system of spelling can perfectly represent the sounds of all the speakers of English, and so we must reconcile ourselves to thinking of phonetic spelling as being a more universal, almost idealized, representation of the language. And considering that our alphabet has 26 letters with which to represent 34 phonemes (the open transition is always represented by a space, appropriately), it does quite well. Some letters do double duty (*c* and *g*), and some phonemes are represented by two- and three-letter combinations (*digraphs* and *trigraphs*). Because of these multi-letter combinations, we will find the linguists' term *phonogram* a more satisfactory one for the symbol representing a single phoneme.

The phonetic alphabet used by most linguists today is a modification of the International Phonetic Alphabet and provides single symbols for all these sounds in English, and will prove much less cumbersome and ambiguous to use than the most frequently employed letters. Actually, most of the common sounds of English are represented in this phonetic alphabet by the usual letter, so that there will not be too many new symbols for the student to learn.

In some ways the consonant sounds of English cause less trouble than the vowels and semivowels. There is less dialectal variation, generally speaking, among the consonants, and some of them are quite regular in their representation in spelling. But consonants are very subject to changes in pronunciation brought on by adapting the mouth to an adjacent sound. A brief discussion here of how these consonant sounds are made will therefore be useful later when we come to discuss these phenomena and their effect upon spelling.

Consonants may be classified in various ways. One, according to whether they are voiced or not; if a sound is voiced, the vocal cords stretched across the larynx are held taut enough to vibrate as the sound is spoken; if it is not voiced, the vocal cords are relaxed and the breath comes through without any vibration in making the sound being spoken. Most of us shift so readily from voiced to unvoiced sounds and back again that we cannot feel any difference between the two in our mouths or throats. But if you will place your thumb on one side of your larynx (Adam's apple) and your first two fingers on the other side, and press gently, then when you say *out loud* the word *leave*, which is made up entirely of voiced sounds, you should feel a vibration in your larynx throughout the word. Now try the word *leaf*, again *out loud*. The /f/ is the unvoiced sound corresponding to the voiced /v/, and you should feel the vibration cease after the vowel if you speak slowly enough. Or stop your ears and speak the same two words slowly aloud, and you should hear the difference. In English all vowels and a majority of consonants are voiced, and (for all practical purposes) all sounds are made on an exhaling breath. This breath, or aspiration as it is called, is more obvious in the voiceless than in the voiced sounds, but is present in all.

Consonants may further be classified according to point of articulation. Although linguists distinguish eleven such positions—they are not agreed amongst themselves on the terminology for them—the simple division into front, middle, and back positions will suffice for us to distinguish the English phonemes. Sounds made in the front of the mouth involve the use of the lips or teeth or both; those in the middle involve the tongue and the roof of the mouth from the ridge of gum just above the teeth (occasionally the back of the

6

teeth themselves) back to the highest point in the roof of the mouth; those in the back involve the tongue and the soft palate or velum.

Finally, consonants are classified according to manner of articulation, and it is from some prominent aspect of this that the consonants take their names. Sounds made with the breath exhaled through the nose, for example, are *nasals;* consonants in which the flow of breath from the lungs is broken are called *stops,* and so on.

The stops make up a third of the consonants in English. Half of them are voiced, and half are voiceless; they go in very neat pairs: /p/ and /b/ are the front stops, with the closure of the flow of air being created by the closing of the lips; /g/ and /k/ are back stops, the closure being created by contact between the back of the tongue and the rear of the roof of the mouth. In the middle are four stops: /d/ and /t/ are similar to the four just discussed, but the closure is created by pressure of the front of the tongue against the ridge of flesh immediately behind the upper teeth. These six stops are called *aspirates,* although the amount of aspiration (a puff of breath) may be slight and does vary. Linguists, for example, can hear a different amount of aspiration in the /p/ sounds in *pin* and *spin,* or in the /t/ sounds in *sting* and *time.* The other two stops, /č/ as in *church* and /ǰ/ as in *judge,* are called *affricates;*[4] they begin with a closure exactly like that of /t/ and /d/ respectively, but the mouth releases the closure slowly enough that a considerable amount of friction from the passing air is heard. These two sounds are easily confused, as we shall see, with /t/ and /d/ when the latter are followed by an unaccented long *u;* the consonants begin to adjust to the back vowel as the closure is being released, thus creating sounds which closely approximate those of /č/ and /ǰ/.

Nine English consonants are spirants, in which there is no closure, but in which a constriction is created which sets the passing air stream into turbulence. These sounds may be classified by type of constriction as well as position. Those in which the opening is predominantly vertical in length are called *slits.* Voiced and voiceless exist for front and middle positions, as Table I shows, but /h/ has no voiced counterpart in the back position. It may come as a surprise to some students that *th* is used to represent two sounds, but if they will compare the *th* (/ð/) in *thin* and *breath* with the *th* (/θ/) in *then* and *breathe,* they should recognize the difference. The openings which are predominantly horizontal (assuming that the speaker is in an upright position) produce sounds which are known as *grooves:* /z/ and /s/ at the middle position will be familiar; /ž/ as represented by the *z* in *azure* or in the last sound in *garage,* and /š/ as in *shoe* or *finish* will merely provide new symbols for already well-known phonemes.

The remaining seven consonants in English are all known as *resonants,* and all are voiced, like the vowels, which they resemble in some ways. The *lateral* resonant, /l/, points the tongue up at the middle of the mouth, making a closure there but allowing the air to slide by on either side with little or no friction. The three *nasals* are all stopped sounds, formed just like the stops except that the closure is held longer and the sound is allowed to reverberate through the nasal cavity and the air to escape through the nose. The sounds are all common, but the symbol /ŋ/ for the final sound in *sing* may be new. The *median* resonants are the ones closest to the vowels; /r/ is occasionally referred to as a semivowel, and as we shall see, /w/ and /y/ are semivowels.

---

[4] Although it is sometimes disputed as to whether /č/ and /ǰ/ are single or double consonant sounds (*x,* for example, represents a double consonant sound, /ks/), we shall treat each as one as English spelling does; we are, after all, primarily interested in spelling.

Table I. Chart of English Consonants and Their Phonetic Symbols

	Front	Middle	Back
Stops			
aspirated			
voiced	/b/	/d/	/g/
voiceless	/p/	/t/	/k/
affricated			
voiced		/ǰ/	
voiceless		/č/	
Spirants			
slit			
voiced	/v/	/ð/	
voiceless	/f/	/θ/	/h/
grooved			
voiced		/z/	/ž/
voiceless		/s/	/š/
Resonants			
lateral (voiced)		/l/	
nasal (voiced)	/m/	/n/	/ŋ/
median (voiced)	/w/	/r/	/y/

Although we do not usually think of long and short consonants as we do of long and short vowels, such a distinction exists. It concerns spelling most directly in the form of double letters, which are actually always pronounced only once, but represent consonants which are held for a longer duration than those represented by a single letter. These double letters cause considerable trouble to unwary spellers who hear only one sound and so write only one letter. We shall try to deal with this problem later, as well as with a lesser one created by a related phenomenon. When two different but closely related sounds are adjacent, they tend to be pronounced as though they were a long form of one of them, as though a double letter and not two different letters appeared in the spelling. For example, *cupboard* is commonly pronounced /kəbərd/; /p/ and /b/ are closely related sounds, differing only in voice, and so the combination /pb/ becomes virtually the same as a long /b/, and we no longer hear the /p/ though we write the *p*. Another example would be *blackguard*, pronounced /blægərd/, in which the /g/ has absorbed the /k/.

The vowels also may be classified in various ways, only one of which is the same as for consonants. Vowels, in English at least, are formed in three parts of the mouth, front, middle, and back, just like the consonants. For example, pronounce the vowel sound of *bit*, with the tip of the finger lightly touching the tongue. Then pronounce the vowel sound of *book*; you should notice that the tip of the tongue has receded, and the back is bunched up in the rear of the mouth. Now try the same thing with the vowel sounds of *bet* and the first syllable of *gonna*, and *bat* and *bought*. Once again you should feel your tongue shift from the front to the back position. The middle position is more difficult to feel, but if you compare the vowels of the words just mentioned with those of the second and third syllables of *halibut* and the first syllable of *bottle*, you may begin to feel the difference as well as hear it.

Of equal importance in creating the vowels is the height of the tongue. Looking into a mirror at the same time if possible, place your thumb and forefinger lightly on the under edge of your chin bone so as to detect any upward or downward movement, and repeat *aloud* the sequence *bit, bet, bat,* or *sit, set, sat.* You should feel your jaw, and probably your tongue too, lower as you progress from high to middle to low. The farther back in the mouth the vowels are formed, the less obvious the change is on the outside, but if you go directly from high to low, pronouncing *book,* then *balk,* or *soot,* then *sought,* you may feel a change even there.

These two aspects of vowel formation are enough to provide the chart of the nine simple vowels of English shown in Table II. Two other aspects are often included, however, and should be mentioned here. The first, lip-rounding, is not particularly important in American English. Most Americans round their lips somewhat for the back vowels, and the more they do so the more distinct the vowel sounds are, but for students of spelling this element seems otherwise to have little importance. The second, the tension of the tongue, may be observed if you will place your first finger across the muscles of your upper throat, about an inch and a half back of the point of the chin, and then say aloud the words *sit* and *seat;* the tension in the vowel of the latter should be noticeably greater. In ordinary speech, differences in tension tend to be leveled out, but in words spoken in isolation as the two above, the distinction remains quite clear, and can be quite useful in distinguishing the simple vowels from the vowel nuclei (to be discussed shortly), as the above example illustrates.

Table II. Chart Showing the Positions and Phonetic Symbols for the Simple Vowels of English

	Front	Middle	Back
High	/i/	/ɨ/	/u/
Middle	/e/	/ə/	/o/
Low	/æ/	/a/	/ɔ/

Some of the phonetic symbols in Table II are the ones most likely to confuse you, so learn them carefully. For example, /a/ is the sound commonly represented by *o;* what we often think of as "short a" is indicated by /æ/. "Short u" has a special symbol, an inverted *e* or *schwa;* /u/ is the sound most commonly represented by *oo.* Three illustrative series of words for these sounds may prove helpful:

High Front (/i/)	pit	sit	bick[er]
Middle Front (/e/)	pet	set	beck
Low Front (/æ/)	pat	sat	back
High Middle (/ɨ/)			
Middle Middle (/ə/)	putt		buck
Low Middle (/a/)	pot	sot	bock
High Back (/u/)	put	soot	book
Middle Back (/o/)			
Low Back (/ɔ/)		sought	balk

As you can see, we have been unable to supply a sequence which provided examples for two of the nine vowels; most speakers of English have only seven vowels in their speech, with the other two being treated as substitutes for or allophones of one of the other vowels.

For example, the vowel known as "barred i" because its phonetic symbol is the letter *i* with a bar across it (/ɨ/), I do not happen to have in my speech; but in the southeastern United States it is very common, and many persons use it to the complete exclusion of /i/, which I employ. Neither the users of my dialect nor the users of the southeastern dialect probably are conscious of using anything but a sound commonly represented by the letter *i*, and so the difference makes little difficulty in spelling; remarks which apply to /i/ apply equally well to /ɨ/. Only occasionally, as in the pronunciation of *just* and *does* by some Americans, does the sound /ɨ/ involve spellings not found for /i/ as well. Many people have both these sounds in their speech, but are quite unconscious of shifting from one to the other—at least so far as their speech is concerned. They are most likely to use the /ɨ/ in unaccented syllables ending in *i* (or *y*), particularly when the *i* stands alone as a syllable (as in *halibut*), or when it is final in the word (words ending in the suffix *-ly* form a very large group of these).

The other dialectal variation is the o-like sound employed by many Americans solely in the first vowel of the contraction *gonna*, and by Down Easters as their characteristic shortening of the so-called long vowel in such words as *whole, home, road,* and *coat*. In general, however, this sound occurs so sporadically that it is not recognized by English spelling. It is represented by the phonetic symbol /o/, and in most cases may be considered an allophone of /a/.

A third simple vowel deserves some notice here though it is illustrated in our sequences above. The "open o" or /ɔ/ appears quite consistently in certain words and is an obvious phoneme. But in some dialects it usurps so much of the work of /a/ that it becomes almost an allophone of that sound! In the coastal areas of New England and some other places, for example, the word *on* is pronounced very much like the first three letters of the word *awning, pond* is pronounced as though spelled *pawned,* and many other words have a similar fate. This sound can also be confused with a vowel nucleus usually spelled *au* or *aw,* so we shall have to discuss it more fully later.

These nine simple vowels can then be combined with each of the three semivowels (/H, w, y/) to form a total of 27 diphthongs or vowel nuclei. If you have access to a tape recorder that can be played backwards, you can discover that the semivowels /w/ and /y/ are the same as the consonants /w/ and /y/ respectively; *say* played backwards gives something very much like *yes,* while *would* played backwards sounds like *do.* The semivowel /H/, however, seems to be different from the consonant, and so qualifies as the 34th phoneme.

The nature of these nuclei has only recently been recognized by linguists themselves; they have certainly not been recognized by English spelling. Yet much of the dialectal variation in the language occurs in these nuclei. No dialect contains all 27, yet every one occurs in at least one American dialect. English spelling has recognized the commonest of them as the so-called "long" vowels, and though it may be inaccurate linguistically to talk of long vowels, we shall find the expression a useful generic one for a group of nuclei which are, so far as English spelling is concerned, allophones. English has provided patterns for nine long vowels; a tabulation of them, with the phonetic symbols for the nuclei which they represent, is given in Table III.

In Table IV we will present a summary of this material in a somewhat different form. The average person does not have many more than nine vowel nuclei in his repertoire of sounds, and the table will suggest why. The blanks are combinations which occur only rarely or in only a few dialects. The missing vowel nuclei with /H/, for example, are most

10

long *a*:	/ey/ as in *day, say,* and *gate*
long *e*:	/iy/, or, in some American dialects (in and around Philadelphia, for example), /iy/, as in *me, bee, see*
long *i*:	/ay/, /æy/, or /ɔy/, as in *tide, dime,* and *pipe*
long *o*:	/ow/, or occasionally /əw/ or /ew/, as in *go, vote* and *home*
long *oo*:	/uw/ as in *food, moon,* and *too*
long *u*:	/iw/ or /iw/. It is often described as being long *oo* preceded by /y/. This vowel nucleus is extremely unstable, and the /i/ appears and disappears from one dialect to another. As minimal pairs can be found which depend upon the presence or absence of this /i/ (*feud* and *food,* for example), and as English spelling seems at times to recognize it, we include it as a legitimate long vowel for consideration with the others.
oi:	/oy/ or /ɔy/, as in *toy, toil, turmoil*
ou:	/æw/ or /aw/, as in *how, house,* and *out*
au:	/oH/ or /ɔH/, as in *lawn, saw,* and *autumn*

clearly heard in New England areas where "the *r* is not pronounced." /əH/ can be heard in this dialect's pronunciation of *first, shirt;* /uH/ in *poor, sure;* /iH/ in *fear, clear;* the so-called "broad a," to many indistinguishable from /a/ except for its prolongation, is /aH/ as in *calm* and *ah.* The other blanks in Table IV all fall into the same category. Most people need only one pronunciation, for example, for such words as *house* or *vote* or *tide,* so that the duplications in the chart generally cause little confusion; the nuclei that are really troublesome to a speller are ones like those just discussed which involve ignoring or slurring the sound represented by a letter in the spelling.

Table IV. Chart of Simple Vowels, Glides, and
Resulting Long Vowels

	/y/	/w/	/H/
/i/	long *e*	long *u*	
/e/	long *a*	long *o*	
/æ/	long *i*	*ou*	
/i/	long *e*	long *u*	
/ə/	*oi*	long *o*	
/a/	long *i*	*ou*	
/u/		long *oo*	
/o/	*oi*	long *o*	*au*
/ɔ/	long *i*		*au*

These long vowels have developed a pattern of sorts in spelling. For each long vowel the usual representation at the end of a syllable other than a final syllable is the single letter, as in *ba·con, se·cret,* and so on. At the end of the final syllable the sound is represented by distinctive phonograms, usually digraphs. In syllables ending in a consonant at least two methods of representation have developed for every vowel, one being the familiar vowel-consonant-silent-*e* combination, the other a digraph followed by the consonant. The former is preferred for final syllables, the latter for other-than-final syllables, with the preference varying in intensity from one vowel to another. Some vowels have also developed a preference for one of these last two phonograms for single-syllable words, using the other for polysyllables. No long vowel, unfortunately, has only these four phonograms. Borrowings from other languages have added extra phonograms, and still more have been added through phonetic changes in English itself. Because the generalizations about the spelling of the long vowels or vowel nuclei are so unreliable, we have chosen to say something about them as a group here rather than wait until we take them up individually later on.

This chapter is in no sense intended to pose as an exhaustive treatment of English phonetics. But if you are going to spell phonetically (as many college students try to without knowing how), you must be able to hear the sounds of English and understand how you make them, so that you can understand some of the phonetic changes which occur in the language and which prove troublesome to spellers. If you have mastered this chapter, and can do the exercises which immediately follow, you should be ready to proceed.

Exercises

Linguists, as we have already said, like to use minimal pairs; we too shall find them very useful. A number of the following exercises are based on minimal pairs of one type or another; the exercises are all designed to help you hear and distinguish the sounds of English better before we begin the spelling itself. We suggest that you not only read the words over *out loud* to yourself, but that you also get someone to read them aloud to you.

1. The first four exercises deal with the eight stops. Those who have the most trouble with them are native speakers of Germanic languages, who either do not have the sound at all in their original speech (/ǰ/, for example), or who do not have it in a position in which it is common in English (German, for example, has no final /d/, a fact which makes the distinction between such words as *hard* and *heart* difficult for a native speaker of that language). The following minimal pairs may help to distinguish the stops:

rip	cup	bid	aid	pat	dart
rib	cub	bit	eight	bat	tart
back	singe	craze	tent	tab	jar
bag	cinch	graze	tend	tap	char
jump	bard	tamp	rend	rumble	tingle
dump	barge	champ	wrench	rumple	tinkle
dodge	joke	pit	patter	dodder	batter
dock	choke	pitch	patcher	dodger	badger

2. Dialectal variations within the United States often create trouble also. That associated with the stops is usually a result of adapting the mouth to articulate a new sound before completing the first one, as in palatalization (which we have already described on p. 7), or when, after a nasal resonant, the nasal passages are closed off too soon and when the mouth is opened it sounds as though a stop formed in the same part of the mouth as the nasal had crept into the word, as in /səmpðiŋ/ for *something*. This latter phenomenon can occur at the end of words also, as in the title of James Whitcomb Riley's "Little Orphant Annie." Pronounce the following to see whether any extra stops creep in that are not in the spelling:

comfort	warmth	dreamt	vermin
margin	drown	singer	conquest

3. A similar phenomenon occurs in adapting the mouth after other sounds than nasals. Do you pronounce an "unspelled" stop at the end of any of the following words?

once	twice	across	worse

4. Look up the derivation of the following words in your dictionary; can you explain the presence in them of a stop following a nasal or an /s/?

against	nimble	peasant	humble	crumb
thunder	astound	hind	pennant	behest

5. The spirants have one peculiarity not shared by other sounds in English; they sometimes (not always) shift from voiced to voiceless (or reverse) to indicate differences in number, part of speech, and so on. This fact can help you learn to distinguish between them. Pronounce aloud the following nouns *and* their correct plurals, and have someone else pronounce them to you, and note what difference, if any, results in the spelling:

life	thief	shelf	sheaf	self
loaf	wolf	wharf	mouth	hoof
sheath	oath	truth	house	vase

6. In the following exercise pronounce aloud and have read to you the nouns and adjectives given *and* the verb forms corresponding to each one. Listen carefully for any changes in sound of the spirant and note any changes in spelling:

safe	belief	sooth	bath	strife
shelf	mouth	advice	cloth	close

7. In this exercise pronounce the pairs of words and have them pronounced to you; notice what happens to the spirant in sound, and note carefully any changes in spelling:

north	south	worth	please
northern	southern	worthy	pleasure

visible	glass	glacier	rouge
vision	glaze	glazier	ruche

8. The ninth spirant we have not mentioned yet in these exercises. It once had a voiced counterpart, /x/, much like the modern German *ch* in *ach,* but that sound disappeared in the sixteenth century, leaving as its chief memento the silent *gh* combination. /h/, itself, is one of the more unstable elements in the language; it is, as Professor Kenyon says, "not so much a sound in itself as it is a manner of beginning various vowel sounds."[5] In all words, the /h/ tends to weaken or disappear in unstressed positions, and in most it tends to be retained in stressed positions. In a few words, initial /h/ has disappeared in general use, though the letter lingers on. In the following lists, the /h/ disappears pretty universally in the first row, frequently (i.e. for many speakers) in the second row, and only in unstressed sentence positions in the third. We will discuss this phenomenon later (Chapter 19), but now test your own tongue and ear on these words:

heir	honest	honor	hour	shepherd	vehicle
herb	hotel	humble	humor	historical	hereditary
huge	hospital	hasten	heal	apprehend	underhanded

You will be interested in the derivation of *able* and *arbor* also.

9. Of the seven resonants, /r/ most closely resembles /h/ in one respect: in many dialects it disappears or appears in a fashion puzzling to those who do not speak one of those dialects. The New

---

[5] John S. Kenyon, *American Pronunciation,* 8th ed., Ann Arbor, Mich., George Wahr, 1940, p. 71.

England version is probably the best known in America, but many people in New York City and vicinity, the South and Southeast, "do not pronounce their r's." This description of their use of /r/ is inaccurate, even though common; these speakers drop the /r/ only before a consonant in the same or a closely following word, or before a pause. Before a vowel they keep the /r/ and occasionally add it when it is not in the spelling, especially after back vowels involving rounding the mouth, as the /ɔH/ of *saw* in "I saw a boat." You should beware of this trait if you speak one of these dialects. Below are a few cases in which the loss or addition of an /r/ has spread beyond dialectal bounds and become almost universal. Pronounce them naturally (in a sentence if possible) and compare your pronunciation with the spelling:

surprise	governor	particular
worsted	comfortable	Saturday

What do you think is the origin of the verbs *bust, cuss, holler?*

10. Like /r/, /l/ represents more than one sound identifiable by linguists. Yet it is only when these sounds disappear and the letters remain, or the sounds appear and the letters are not present, that spelling trouble arises. This fact will, perhaps, make it easier for us to understand the speakers of some Oriental languages which make no phonemic distinction between /l/ and /r/; these people have considerable difficulty with these sounds in English. You might try your own ear and tongue on these minimal or near-minimal pairs:

chatter	little	red	solely
chattel	litter	led	sorely
late	faulty	forage	firing
rate	forty	foliage	filing

11. As we have seen, /w/ and /y/ are both glides, or semivowels. They always have to be used in conjunction with another vowel. When they follow the vowel, they create a diphthong or vowel nucleus, and may or may not be represented in the spelling, as we shall see when we get to the long vowels. When they precede the vowel, they are for convenience sake considered consonants, although fundamentally the same sounds. As consonants they are occasionally not represented in the spelling, or at least not in the orthodox fashion (i.e. not by *w*, or by *i* or *y*). A few of these words which are common may help you to recognize the sound and be on guard for the spelling:

one	unit	beauty	going	go on
feud	eulogy	cube	accumulate	language

12. As we have said, people who do not regularly use /ɨ/ in their speech are most likely to use it in words where an *i* (or *y*) stands alone as an unaccented syllable, or occasionally when it stands at the end of an unaccented syllable, following a consonant. It may help you in your spelling if you can detect, in the following words, the difference in the sound represented by *i* from either /i/ or /ə/.

halibut	similar	organization	indivisibility
comical	familiar	heretical	horrible
capital	regiment	exhibition	initial

13. The preceding exercises have dealt with consonant sounds; the remaining ones will test your ability to deal with vowel sounds. Below are some minimal pairs to help you hear the difference between the simple vowels and long vowels; the first word in each group contains the short or simple vowel, and the second (and third and fourth if such are given) contains the long one:

pat	bed	bit	hop	cub
pate	bead	bite	hope	cube
frat	said	kit	got	jut
freight	seed	kite	goat	jute

14

past	met	sit	rod	mud
paste	meat	sight	road	mewed
paced	meet	site	rode	
	mete	cite		
mat	stead	tip	doll	mud
mate	steed	type	dole	mood
mad	etch	pill	lob	mutt
made	each	pile	lobe	mute
lack	less	his	clock	mutt
lake	lease	hies	cloak	moot
		highs		
pant	bend	ill	slop	fug
paint	beaned	isle	slope	fugue
		aisle		
bran	sedge	whit	cox	spud
brain	siege	white	coax	spewed
brass	wretch	flit	sock	rut
brace	reach	flight	soak	root

14. We will learn before long that the length of the vowel in a one-syllable word may influence the spelling of the consonant following it. As some words have suffered a shortening of their long vowel in various American dialects, you need to beware of this. Are the following pairs of words rhyming words for you, or only minimal pairs, with a long vowel in the first word and a short vowel in the second?

creek	whole	home	breeches (plural)
crick	hull	hum	britches

sleek	clique
slick	click

15. In some of the following pairs there is a shift of accent as well as of vowel length; mark the long vowel in each pair:

outpass	secret	critic	coma	a sum (2 words)
outpace	secrete	critique	comma	assume

16. The following are phonetic transcriptions of some common words, to give you practice in using our set of symbols. After each one write the correct spelling in the usual English alphabet:

/čərč/ _____   /jǝj/ _____   /buk/ _____   /θæt/ _____   /ðiŋ/ _____

/kæč/ _____   /fiš/ _____   /gɔlf/ _____   /kuk/ _____   /hæv/ _____

/šæl/ _____   /breð/ _____   /keyk/ _____   /θen/ _____   /jist/ _____

/geyj/ _____   /šuw/ _____   /fayv/ _____   /diyd/ _____   /voys/ _____

/stap/ _____   /mayn/ _____   /hoHl/ _____   /haws/ _____   /gəraž/ _____

/klow'·žuwr/ _____   /siŋ'·iŋ/ _____   /oHn'·iŋ/ _____   /ney'·zəl/ _____   /spay'·rənt/ _____

2

Syllable Division, Roots, and Affixes

Most of us have had the experience, I think, of coming to the end of a line of writing and finding our word only half finished. Repeated pronunciations made it seem as though the syllable division could come in either one of two places in the word. This is probably the result of a spelling-induced pronunciation of the word in isolation, for one thing. And it is also the result of a fundamental misconception of what a syllable is.

The vowel and consonant sounds in English differ from one another in sonorousness, that is, in the amount of sound that each one has. This varies not merely from being spoken *sotto voce* to being shouted, but from the very nature of the sound itself. The least sonorous sound of all, for example, is /h/. In general a voiced consonant is more sonorous than a voiceless one; any vowel sound is more sonorous than a consonant sound.

In addition to its sonorousness, the sound in a word acquires what is loosely called accent. This is a combination of the variation in stress within the word, and the changing stress and pitch resulting from the sentence meaning and speaker's emotion. The combination of sonorousness and accent is called intensity, and the ups and downs of intensity create syllables in the spoken language, with the most intense point being the center of the syllable. Because of its greater sonorousness, a vowel sound will usually appear in most syllables, but this is not always the case. For example, in the slow, carefully articulated language of a church service, *heaven* is usually a two-syllable word; the final /e/ is made sonorous enough and accented enough to be what is called the "syllabic." In ordinary, everyday speech the /e/ is slurred over and the /n/ becomes the syllabic: /hev·'n/. If the /n/ is made more sonorous than the /v/, the word becomes a one-syllable word.

The low point of intensity marks the change from one syllable to another. This point may, and often does, fall between two sounds, but it may also fall in the middle of a sound, as may be illustrated with what are commonly called the long consonants. These are frequently represented by double letters which, as we have already pointed out, represent only one sound, as in *illegal*. Convention dictates that in writing, the syllable divisions be made between double letters, which is quite correct, for the division in speech comes in the middle of the long consonant sound which the letters represent. In speech, therefore, it is a misconception to feel that every sound "goes" with one syllable or another.

When this syllable division falls in the middle of a long consonant represented by a single letter, however, the result may be puzzling to the student not only for syllabication but for spelling as well. The word *prejudice* provides a good example. The syllable division falls in the middle of the sound represented by the letter *j;* the part of the sound which goes with the preceding syllable sounds vaguely like /d/ (see the discussion of /ǰ/ on page 7), and so many an unwary student has misspelled the word by writing *predjudice*.[1] This

---

[1] Linguists, in using hypothetical forms or forms not known to exist, always mark them with an asterisk (*); we shall use the same device on those rare occasions when we wish to write out misspellings for you.

16

situation is most likely to occur after a prefix ending in a vowel which has changed from a complex to a simple sound, and may involve incorrectly doubling a letter, as in the misspelling *prefference*. An awareness of word structure, of which we shall have something to say later in this chapter, is the best defense against this type of error.

In writing, certain conventions have been developed, largely by printers. A majority of the time (though far from universally) these happen to coincide with syllable divisions in speech, and so are useful in spelling as well as in dividing words at the end of a line. These conventional "guides" (as we prefer to call them rather than "rules") to syllable division we present below, along with some other information which you may find useful:

I. When *one* consonant sound seems to stand alone between two vowel sounds, and there is a question as to which syllable it goes with, the following generalizations will be helpful:

1. If the first vowel is *short* and *accented,* the consonant probably goes with it:

mod est	civ il	leg end	butch er
val en tine	un cov er	cav al cade	cyl in der

2. If the first vowel sound is *long* and *accented,* the chances are that the consonant goes with the second vowel:

ri val	mu sic	pi lot	vo cal
dy nas ty	po ten tate	cu cum ber	ve lum

3. Regardless of its length, if the *second* vowel is *accented,* the consonant probably goes with it:

hu mane	re gard	ga rage	pa rade
e las tic	do mes tic	e nig ma	de moc ra cy

You should note, however, that an open vowel (i.e. a vowel sound which concludes a syllable) in an unaccented syllable loses some of its length. Both /ey/ and /ay/ become short sounds (/ə/ and /i/ respectively, usually), while /iy/, /ow/, /uw/ and /iw/, although retaining something of the quality which makes them "long" vowels, are held a shorter time than the corresponding accented vowels.

4. When *both* the vowels in question are *unaccented,* the consonant usually goes with the second:

men di cant	clas si fy	bach e lor
trip li cate	met ri cal	hal i but

You should remember that we are dealing here with sounds, and that when those sounds are represented by digraphs and trigraphs, the clusters of letters are treated as one letter. We shall soon encounter four such groups (*ch, tch, dge,* and, when the silent *e* disappears before suffixes, *dg*), and later we will meet *ph, th, sh, ck,* and others. When these represent one sound they are never separated for syllable division. Sometimes, of course, in compound words the two letters happen to come together, as in *porthole, uphill,* and *mishap,* but this type of word is easy to identify.

Other sequences of consonant letters will represent two or more sounds, and be treated somewhat differently. Do you, for example, remember ever seeing an English word beginning with the letters *ft*? This sequence is common enough at the end of English words, as in *aft* and *heft.* When two or more consonants are pronounced together in this way in a syllable, they are called a "blend," and it is part of the patterning of the English language to use these blends, for the most part, either at the beginning of syllables only, or at the end of syllables only. And as these two groups of blends are treated differently in syllable division, it is useful to be able to distinguish between them readily. Table V is a chart of the commonest blends (as you can see from the blanks in the chart, only about one seventh of the mathematically possible two-consonant blends exist in English).[2]

Table V. Common Blends of English Consonants

Initial in Syllables

	/b/	/d/	/f/	/g/	/h/	/k/	/p/	/s/	/š/	/t/	/ð/
/k/								/sk/			
/l/	/bl/		/fl/	/gl/		/kl/	/pl/	/sl/			
/m/								/sm/			
/n/								/sn/			
/p/								/sp/			
/r/	/br/	/dr/	/fr/	/gr/		/kr/	/pr/	/st/	/šr/	/tr/	/ðr/
/t/											
/w/		/dw/			/hw/	/kw/		/sw/		/tw/	

Three-phoneme blends: /skr/, /skw/, /spl/, /spr/, /str/.

Final in Syllables

	/b/	/č/	/d/	/f/	/ǰ/	/k/	/l/	/m/	/n/	/p/	/s/	/t/	/ð/	/v/
/d/													/dð/	
/f/											/fs/	/ft/	/fð/	
/k/											/ks/	/kt/		
/l/	/lb/	/lč/	/ld/	/lf/	/lǰ/	/lk/		/lm/	/ln/	/lp/	/ls/	/lt/	/lð/	/lv/
/m/										/mp/	/ms/			
/n/		/nč/	/nd/		/nǰ/						/ns/	/nt/	/nð/	
/ŋ/						/ŋk/								
/p/											/ps/	/pt/		
/r/	/rb/	/rč/	/rd/	/rf/	/rǰ/	/rk/	/rl/	/rm/	/rn/	/rp/	/rs/	/rt/	/rð/	/rv/
/s/						/sk/				/sp/		/st/		
/z/								/zm/						

Three-phoneme blends: /ksð/, /lfð/, /mpt/, /mpf/, all uncommon. We have made no attempt to include blends made by inflectional -s.

A few comments on these groups of blends may be helpful before we go on. You will notice that /sk/, /sp/, and /st/ are the only blends to appear in both lists, and that in the list of final blends, they are the only ones involving /s/ in which this sound is the first. Because of their vowel-like quality, the resonants, particularly /l/ and /r/, are the most frequent elements in the blends. In initial blends the resonant is the second (or third) element; in final blends the resonant is the first element (or both elements). The only exception to this last statement is the blend /zm/, which is always written *sm*, as is the initial blend /sm/. Here, however, the sound will tell you which blend you are dealing with.

---

[2] We have listed almost 60 blends; students wishing to see a complete listing of linguistically possible blends in English should consult Benjamin Lee Whorf, *Language, Thought, and Reality*, New York, John Wiley & Sons, 1956, p. 223.

Similarly, the stops are the first part of initial blends except when following /s/ (a spirant), and the last part of final blends except when followed by /s/ or another stop (as in the blend /pt/, for example). The one exception to this last statement is an interesting one, the blend /dð/, which does not appear in many words and does not have the usual /d/, made, as we have seen, by putting the tip of the tongue against the ridge of flesh just above the teeth. When you say *width* or *breadth* rapidly in a sentence, you anticipate the /ð/ by making the /d/ with your tongue against your teeth. This fact is of little importance for spelling except to point out again the fact that as long as no phonemic difference is involved, it is perfectly feasible to have one letter represent two sounds.

Some of the blanks on the chart were once active blends. We shall see that *pt* can begin a word (*ptomaine,* for example); it can also end a word (*apt*). But as we shall discover, when *pt* begins a word, the *p* is silent. This is what is known as a "fossil blend"—only the written shell remains of a formerly live spoken blend of sounds. One way in which the language shows signs of continued growth and change, of course, is in these alterations in its blends. Some have even disappeared from the language. Chantecleer, in Chaucer's *Canterbury Tales,* for example, describes murder as being "wlatsom" (i.e. nauseating), using a blend no longer used initially in English. Again, in the *Canterbury Tales,* Chaucer says that the Cook's head cold makes him "fnesen" (i.e. sniffle); /fn/ is no longer used as a blend in English.

II. We should now turn to our second guide to syllabication, for a blend standing between two vowels:

1. A final blend (so called because always seen most characteristically when final in a word) is always divided between the two syllables, regardless of length of vowel or accent concerned:

sys tem	cam pus	van dal
car pen ter	or der ly	in ter val

2. An initial blend follows much the same pattern as a *single* consonant between vowels (compare the following with guide I):

a. If the first vowel sound is *short* and *accented,* it draws one of the consonants to it, and the blend is divided:

ac rid	pop lin	gob let
sym met ric	trip li cate	in teg ri ty

b. If the first vowel sound is *long* and *accented,* the blend goes with the second vowel:

mi grate	se cret	cy clist
ca the dral	re du pli cate	tes ta trix

c. Regardless of its length, if the *second* vowel is *accented,* the blend will go with it:

ne glect	a sleep	de tract
li bret to	pro cliv i ty	re frig er ate

d. When *both* vowels are *unaccented,* the blend will go with the second:

ver te brate	pic to graph	ther mo stat
in te gral	mul ti pli ca tion	

III. Three-consonant blends are few in number; we have listed the commonest in Table V. They behave in general as do two-consonant blends. In the case of initial blends, only one consonant goes to the first syllable when the blend is divided:

il lus trious	an tis tro phe	il lu stra tion

Final blends, except for /mpt/, seem generally to appear at the end of a word where syllable division is not a problem; /mpt/ follows the rule for final two-consonant blends, with the division coming between the /mp/ and the /t/:

pre emp tive   emp ty   per emp to ry

There are, of course, many two- and three-consonant sequences which are not blends. In the case of the two-consonant sequences, the division will obviously fall between the two sounds:

ob ject   nut meg   pit fall   dog ma

With three-consonant sequences, the division will come between a blend and a single sound. The only time this might be confusing is when the first two consonants make a final blend, and the second and third form an initial blend. In that situation the initial blend is preserved, as in *pan·try* and *per·spire*.

IV. Words with four or more consonant sounds between two vowels are primarily compound words or words with affixes, so that the structure of the word makes the syllabication clear:

con struct   land scape   hand spring   cork screw

Words may be divided not only into syllables, but also into roots, prefixes, and suffixes (the last two known collectively as affixes). The main idea of a word is carried in the root, which is rarely more than two syllables long (except for compound words where two words have been joined to make a new one). As Lancelot Hogben says, these roots are the foundation-brick of language.[3]

There are times, however, when it is desirable to add to or modify this basic meaning in some way, and one common method of doing so in English is through the use of prefixes and suffixes. What these affixes contribute to the meaning may vary all the way from merely indicating the part of speech of the word (as *-ly* sometimes does) to making it mean the opposite of what it did (as *un-* sometimes does). Also, the language tends, in popular usage (and particularly with non-native roots) to limit or "specialize" the meaning of the root when prefixes and suffixes are added. As we shall have occasion later to single out the Latin root *ject,* from *jectus,* the past participle of *jacere,* to throw, we shall use it as an example here. Below are several common words with *ject* in them, and what would be a literal translation of the Latin elements. Compare these translations with the narrower limits imposed by usage on these words; words with *ject* cannot be used anywhere that *throw* could be, even though the dictionary probably allows for wider usage than does your experience with the word:

abject   —throw away
deject   —throw down
eject   —throw out
inject   —throw in
interject —throw between or among
project   —throw forward
reject   —throw back
subject   —throw under

---

[3] Lancelot Hogben (ed.), *The Loom of Language,* by Frederick Bodmer, New York, W. W. Norton, 1944, p. 38.

Take a sheet of paper and see how many other words you can make with *ject,* either with other prefixes, or by adding or varying the suffixes. Notice how the specialization of the idea of "throw" varies from word to word.

Some of this word building took place in Roman times, and we have inherited the entire word, root, prefix, and suffix. In other words the combining may have been done somewhere *en route* to present-day English: in Late Latin, in Old French, in Middle English, or in Early Modern English. Many of these Latin roots, prefixes, and suffixes are still very much alive today and are still being used to build new English words. And the same procedure, of course, applies to native English roots (cf. *man, manly, manliness, unmanly*) and to any other roots adopted by the language.

With the usual exercises, we have put at the end of this chapter a list of common Latin roots and (mostly Latin) prefixes and suffixes, in the hope that you will gradually become familiar with them and their meanings. The value of such word study in vocabulary building should be obvious; combined with wide reading it is one of the surest ways of increasing one's vocabulary. And it has its value for the speller as well. A knowledge of whether or not a certain syllable in a word is an affix or not can be useful; there are other advantages also to knowing something of word structure.

Ninety per cent of all the double letters in English are the result of either the assimilation of prefixes ending in consonants, or the doubling of final consonants before suffixes beginning with vowels. We will deal with assimilation first, and then try to cope with the problems sometimes presented by adding suffixes.

Assimilation is the practice of modifying the sound of a final consonant in a prefix when it is placed before another consonant. For example, the prefix *in-*, meaning "not," appears recognizably in such words as *inactive* and *incapable,* but before some sounds it changes, creating such combinations as *illegal, irregular, imbalance, immovable, impractical.* Where a double letter is not created, the change usually causes little trouble in spelling. But the double letters are a nuisance, and are continually tripping students up. They are, of course, particularly troublesome when the root has not been taken into English as an independent word, or is not common enough (as is *ject*) to be easily identified—for example, *arrive.* We give below examples of the seven commonest prefixes which assimilate; there are others, but they involve fewer words and should be learned as you need them after you have mastered these:

---

ad- remains unchanged before *d, h, j, m, v.*
becomes *a-* before *sc, sp,* and *st:*

| ascribe | | aspect | | astringent |

alters as follows before other consonants:

| accord | affect | aggravate | allot | announce |
| appoint | acquaint | arrest | assent | attempt |

---

com- remains unchanged before *b, m,* and *p.*
becomes *con-* before other consonants except *l* and *r.*
changes as follows before *l* and *r:*

| collide | | correct |

---

en-	remains unchanged except before *b, p, ph:*		
embroil		empurple	emphasis

ex-	remains unchanged before *c, h, p, q, s, t.* becomes *e-* before other consonants except *f.* changes as follows before *f:*	
effect		

in-	remains unchanged except before *b, l, m, p, r:*			
imbue	illegal	immovable	import	irregular

ob-	remains unchanged except before *c, f,* and *p:*		
occur		offend	oppose

sub-	remains unchanged except as follows:			
succeed	suffer suspect	suggest	summon sustain	support

Here is a list of twenty of the commonest prefixes in English; look them up in your dictionary (most of them have more than one possible meaning), and familiarize yourself with their usage:

ab-	ad-	be-
com-	de-	dis-
en-	ex-	in- (really 2 prefixes)
inter-	mis-	ob-
per-	post-	pre-
pro-	re-	sub-
trans-	un-	

And here is a list of the commonest suffixes in English. Through your dictionary and through using them, you should familiarize yourself with the meanings of the following:

-able	-ance (-ancy)	-al
-an	-ant	-ate
-cy	-ed	-ence (-ency)
-ent	-er (2)	-est
-fic	-ful	-fy
-ible	-ic (-ical)	-ice
-ile	-ine	-ing
-ish	-ism	-ist
-ity	-ive	-ize
-less	-ly	-ment
-ness	-ous	-sion
-tion	-ty	-y

On the next page we have listed for you some of the commonest Latin roots in English. As the most useful Latin roots are those taken from verbs, and as most English words derived from verbs come from either the infinitive or the past participle, we list only those two principle parts of each Latin verb, along with the form in which it most frequently appears in English and with illustrations:

22

capere, captus	_____	cap, capt cept		capable, captive accept, except
(from a late form, *ceptus*:)				
cedere, cessum	_____	cede, ceed, cess		accede, exceed, excess
ducere, ductus	_____	duce, duct		deduce, induct
facere, factus	_____	**face, fact**		**face, fact, facile** factitious
(a later form of the same verb:) ficere, fectus	_____	fice, fect		suffice, effect
ferre, latus	_____	fer, late		confer, collate
jacere, jectus	_____	jac, ject		ejaculate, eject
legere, lectus	_____	lege, lect		legend, lectern
mittere, missus	_____	mit(t), mise		permit, promise
pendere, pensus	_____	pend, pense		suspend, suspense
plicare, plicatus	_____	plic, plicat(e)		explicit, implicate
ponere, positum	_____ pone (pound), posit			component, compound composition
portare, portatus	_____	port		import
scribere, scriptum	_____	scribe, script		describe, inscription
specere, spectus	_____	spect		suspect, specter
tendere, tentus	_____	tend, tent		attend, attention
tenere, tentus	_____	tain, tent		sustain, content
venire, ventus	_____	vene, vent		convene, convent
vertere, versus	_____	vert, verse		revert, reverse
vivere, victus	_____	vive, viv		revive, vivid

If you do not know the meanings of these Latin roots, look up the English examples in the dictionary; in most dictionaries the derivation will give you the meaning of the original Latin word. Write it in after the word above.

Exercises

The first four exercises are lists of words for you to try your hand on at syllabication. In each case mark the syllable division by a vertical line *between* two letters (do this neatly

—not with a line *through* one letter), and mark the vowel in the accented syllable in each word.

1. This is an exercise for Guide I; remember to mark the accented syllable as well as the syllable division in each word:

bacon	lady	become	rely	rival
radish	wagon	lemon	duty	music
silent	hotel	motion	second	figure
river	holiday	robin	punish	lyric
bachelor	habit	pilot	civil	fracas
tripod	legend	judging	bonus	seven
unit	origin	horizon	eleven	uniform
regulate	episode	modify	municipal	dilatory

2. In this exercise you are to apply guide II; remember to separate the syllables neatly:

reply	rifle	bestir	vibrate	oblige
vandal	candid	costume	compete	sublime
selfish	distort	western	tunnel	darken
pepper	burner	pencil	rusty	doctor
respond	rafter	cyclist	artist	sharpen
verbal	reflex	impish	migrate	happen

3. This will test you on guide III (and give you a little review on guides I and II also):

swiftly	explode	irksome	emblem	extreme
pantry	implore	engrave	surprise	prescriptive
describe	pilgrim	restraint	resplendent	proscription
monster	sixthly	partner	embrace	restriction
preemptive		injunction		contemptuous

4. Here is some practice with guide IV:

obstruct	subscribe	cornflower	promptly	handspring
marksman	campstool	seamstress	unstrung	corkscrew

5. After each of the following words write in the *un*assimilated form of the prefix in the word. A few of the prefixes involved are not in the list of seven which we dealt with in detail on page 40; these words you may have to look up in your dictionary. The others should be easy:

collect _____   suspend _____   aggrieve _____

apprehend _____   transcript _____   corrode _____

embattled _____   ejaculate _____   apposite _____

traduce _____   avocation _____   irrigate _____

offer _____   arrive _____   traverse _____

illiterate _____   amanuensis _____   avert _____

associate _____   conjecture _____

As most good dictionaries have a section on spelling which includes the important rules for spelling changes which occur when suffixes are used, study it, and then do the remaining exercises—they will be easy if you have studied your dictionary well.

6. What conditions must a *one-syllable* word meet in order to double its final consonant before adding a suffix beginning with a vowel (including the suffix *-y*)? Write them in the blanks below:

a. _____

b. _____

c. If your dictionary gives you this information, write here the one one-syllable word which is occasionally an exception:

_____

7. What conditions must a *polysyllabic* word meet in order to double its final consonant before a suffix beginning with a vowel? Write them in the blank spaces below:

a. _____

b. _____

c. _____

d. What is the apparent explanation of the irregular behavior of the following words:

inference (cf. inferring)   deferent (cf. deferred)
preferable (cf. preferring)   referee (cf. referred)

e. What, if anything, does your dictionary have to say about this group of words?

_____

_____

f. What is the explanation of the irregularity (in some cases the allowance of either single or double consonants) in the following words:

benefited or benefitted   programing or programming
humbugged, humbugging   worshiper or worshipper

_____

_____

g. A large number of words end in *l* preceded by a vowel, but with the accent not on the last syllable. Should you treat these words normally in forming derivatives, or are they a special group?

_____

_____

_____

_____

Consider these pairs, both parts of which may be found in good writing:

appareled and apparelled   medalist and medallist
dialing and dialling   gamboling and gambolling

h. What is the source of all this confusion?

_____

_____

8. In general, double letters already at the end of the words remain whether the suffix begins with a consonant or a vowel, but British and American usage also differ about retaining *ll* at the end of words before suffixes. Underline the words in the following group which are the preferred American spellings:

instalment	willfulness	enthrallment	skilful
enrollment	dullness	fulfillment	fulness

9. a. Below the following words write the proper spelling of that word after you have added either *-able* or *-ous:*

advantage	manage	notice	peace
service	outrage	trace	entice

_____

b. Are these spellings what you expect in adding suffixes beginning with vowels onto words ending with a silent *e?*

_____

c. Why?

_____

d. Below the following words write the proper spelling of that word after you have added the suffix *-ing:*

see	hoe	dye	singe	tinge
agree		toe		shoe

_____

e. Why are these words irregular about adding suffixes beginning with a vowel?

_____

f. British and American usage differ again over retaining the silent *e* in one group of words. In the following group, underline those spelled according to American usage:

abridgment	acknowledgment	fledgeling	judgment

g. Make a generalization to fit these words.

_____

_____

_____

h. There are a lot of verbs one syllable long and ending in *-ie*, like *die, lie,* and *tie.* What happens when you add the suffix *-ing* to them? Write some illustrations here:

_____

_____

_____

10. Words ending in *y* preceded by a consonant usually change the *y* to *i* before adding any suffix except one beginning with *i* or the possessive *'s.* The following exercises will help you with the commonest:

   a. Inspect the following words, and then below them write out your generalization as to what type of word is exceptional and when:

shier	shiest	shyly	shyness
slier	sliest	slyly	slyness
sprier	spriest	spryly	spryness
drier	driest	dryly	dryness
wrier	wriest	wryly	wryness

_____

_____

   b. What happens to words ending in *-y* preceded by a consonant when *-like* or *-ship* is added? Think of some examples, look them up in the dictionary, and write down your conclusion below. If you can't think of any examples, try adding *-like* to *city* and *lady,* and *-ship* to *lady* and *secretary.* Your generalization:

_____

_____

11. In a word ending in *-y* preceded by a vowel, there is usually no change before any suffix. The commonest exceptions are listed below, and should be learned as demons, which some of them are. One or two of them have more regular forms permitted; beneath these words write that permitted form (look it up first):

   daily   gaily   said   paid   slain   gluier   gaiety

_____

12. a. Below the following words write the same word with the suffix *-ed* or *-ing* added:

   panic   picnic   shellac   arc   disc

_____

   b. What alteration occurs in the spelling of the original word?

_____

   c. Why does this change take place?

_____

   d. When does it take place?

_____

27

13. One of the commonest stumbling blocks in spelling is the derivative or compound word, the first element of which ends in the same letter with which the second element begins, as *real + ly →* *really, team + mate → teammate,* and *drunken + ness → drunkenness.* Combine the following pairs of word elements into a correctly spelled new word:

room + mate →   stubborn + ness →
usual + ly →   tail + less →
mean + ness →   cool + ly →

3

On Using the Dictionary

One afternoon recently a boy came into my office for his regular conference connected with the freshman composition course. I could tell by the expression on his face and the unusual eagerness with which he began the discussion of his latest theme that he had found something which he wanted very much to tell me about. Sure enough, when we came to the right page, he pointed to a word, *populous,* which I had underlined and marked wrong for spelling, and said triumphantly, "There! That word is spelled correctly. I looked it up before I wrote out the paper, and I've looked it up again since you handed it back." He was rather crestfallen when he read aloud the meanings of *populous* given in the dictionary, and then, at my request, read what the dictionary had to say about *populace,* the word he had wanted to use. His was only one of many examples of the commonest error in using the dictionary for a spelling—not reading far enough. It is not adequate, especially if you are uncertain of the spelling, to stop with the bold-faced type of the word itself.

Although most publishers of dictionaries print little pamphlets on how to use a dictionary, one of which you may have by writing to them for it, we may profitably look at the dictionary ourselves for a moment now. In most standard dictionaries there are "guide words" at the top of each page, indicating the first word alphabetically to appear on that page, and the last word. You should know your alphabet well enough so that you can tell at a glance whether or not your word is on the page before you, or whether you turn forward or backward to find it. Knowing your alphabet will save you a lot of time in the dictionary, which is one of the greatest aids a poor speller has—though it should be used with discretion, and not allowed to become a crutch which will interfere with the ultimate healing of your disability.

When you come to your word, you will find it printed in bold-faced type, with the syllables separated from each other (if there are more than one) by accent marks or by raised periods. Do not mistake the latter for hyphens; look up a word which you know to be hyphenated (most of the words employing *self* as a prefix, for example, are hyphenated) and compare it with other words on the same page having a raised period. The accent mark follows the accented syllable in most dictionaries.

After the word itself comes the pronunciation, enclosed in parentheses and expressed in phonetic symbols which are explained at the foot of the page or at the beginning of the book. As we have already indicated, because of dialectal variations and because dictionaries vary in their methods of dividing words into syllables, these pronunciations may not seem to be the way in which you usually pronounce the word. The dictionary's pronunciation, however, will at least indicate how many people pronounce the word and may be relied upon as an acceptable pronunciation. Following the example of the dictionaries, we put words and letters into phonetic symbols between virgules or slanted lines (another type of parenthesis) when referring to them as sounds, but instead of bold-faced type, we use italic type when referring to them as words or letters.

Following the pronunciation comes an indication of the part of speech by abbreviations in italic type; when a word may be used as two or more different parts of speech, the second abbreviation will appear after the definitions of the word for the first part of speech, and there will be different sets of definitions for each part of speech. My student would have been helped had he gone far enough in his reading of the dictionary to notice that *populous* is an adjective, and had he remembered that he wanted a noun.

Next comes, in some dictionaries, a note of any irregularities in inflectional endings—anything unusual about the formation of the plural of nouns, the participles and preterit of verbs, or the comparative and superlative of adjectives. If these are perfectly normal, you proceed directly to the derivation of the word, which can be extremely helpful to a speller. As we shall see, for example, if you can remember that a word is of Greek origin, that is, either derived from Greek roots or borrowed directly from a Greek word, you may be relatively sure that /f/ will usually be spelled *ph*. And as we go along we shall see a number of other examples in which some ability to recognize a word's derivation will pay handsome dividends to the speller.

Then come the definitions of the words, the recordings of the various meanings each has acquired during its life in the language. And just as in vocabulary building one has not really added a new word to his vocabulary until he can spell it, so one cannot say that he has added one more correct spelling to his list of words mastered until he knows how to use the word with a correct meaning. *The Oxford English Dictionary*, the great historical dictionary, arranges the definitions in the order in which each meaning seems to have appeared in the language, the earliest first. Thus the often fascinating series of changes made by usage in a word's fundamental meaning may be easily followed. Some of our American dictionaries follow this practice also (*Webster's New Collegiate*, for example), whereas others prefer to put first the meaning in most common usage today (*The American College Dictionary*, for example), or to place the most general meaning first and the most specific last (as in *Webster's New World Dictionary*).

Students with weak vocabularies are generally poor spellers; they are continually being put in the situation of having to spell words they do not know or have only half learned. And their troubles are aggravated even further by the number of homonyms in the language, that is, words that sound alike but which have different meanings and may be spelled differently. Many languages, including English, show a tendency, as they develop, to depend almost entirely upon one-syllable words. English has reached the point where most of its everyday words are either monosyllabic, or based on one-syllable words or roots to which prefixes and suffixes may be freely added. Chinese, and a few other southeastern Asiatic languages, have become practically monosyllabic. This shortening of longer words into one-syllable ones has led inevitably to the creation of homonyms. And in English the fondness of its users for borrowing foreign words has complicated the situation further.

In Chinese this profusion of homonyms has not created any spelling problems, for each word has its own symbol, and alphabetic writing is not used. In speech, however, it has created problems for the Chinese language, which has developed a method of using pitch to distinguish between different meanings which would otherwise sound the same. This creates a pattern of pitch so very different from that of English that a native speaker of English, trying to learn Chinese as a second language, probably finds it more difficult than English spelling! In English, however, the difficulty is a written one. With fewer homonyms in general, the speaker of English can usually rely on the context of his sentence to make clear which meaning is intended. It is only when he comes to choose the correct spelling for his homonym in writing that he runs into difficulty.

The problem of learning to use homonyms, therefore, is not entirely a spelling one; it is also a matter of vocabulary, and requires the student to know the different meanings of the words as well as the related spellings. And just as annoying as these true homonyms are the words which are so similar in sound that they affect spellers in the same way. Homonyms and near-homonyms can be classified and, as it is helpful to know what to guard against, we shall deal with them by classification when we get to the exercises.

Finally, you must remember that the word entries are only part of the valuable material offered by the editors of your dictionary. What may loosely be called "preliminary matter" (although some of it comes at the end of some dictionaries) is almost as helpful and interesting to the speller. The "Rules of Spelling" or "Orthography," the "Vocabulary of Rhymes" (if your dictionary has one), "Arbitrary Signs and Symbols," and other sections to which you will be sent in the exercises you will find thoroughly useful.

Exercises

1. Most dictionaries have two guides or keys to pronunciation, a short one and a long one. Find both of them in your dictionary and write in the page references below:

_____

2. Imagine that you are looking at a new calendar, wondering what those funny men-in-the-moon on each page represent. Where in your dictionary can you find out? Name the section and give the page reference below:

_____

3. The apostrophe causes a lot of spelling mistakes (do *you* know the difference between *its* and *it's*, and which is which?); where in your dictionary can you learn how to use it?

_____

4. List below the abbreviations used in your dictionary for the eight parts of speech, and where you found them. (You should not have thumbed through your dictionary until you found an example of each!)

_____

5. Look up the etymology of the word *creole* and explain below all the abbreviations used.

_____

_____

_____

6. Many homonyms are the result of keeping two different phonograms for a long vowel in order to distinguish the written form as well as the meaning of the words (this custom makes reading easier but spelling more difficult). Under the following words write as many homonyms as you can discover, making sure that you know the meaning of every word:

coarse	meet	peace	road	lone
bore	toe	sore	grown	flea
tee	thrown	frieze	weak	steal
read	seem	peal	shone	plane

7. Other homonyms result from the fact that some consonants can be represented in more than one way. Many of these words, however, help the speller by shifting the accent, and hence are really near-homonyms. Under the following words write as many homonyms or near-homonyms as you know for each one, making sure you know the meaning of every word:

assent	descent	past	personal

8. Differences between short vowels are often so slight that they create confusion even between words which are only similar but not identical in pronunciation. The largest group of true homonyms in this classification is that involving the /ər/ combination of sounds. Complete these pairs of easily confused words, looking up the meanings of all:

altar	miner	complement	council	than	berth

9. Other homonyms or pairs of easily confused words are created because two prefixes (at least one of them usually assimilated) sound much alike. Under each of these words write the one with which it is readily confused, being sure you know the meaning of both:

accept	illicit	effect	emigrate	eminent	excess	illusion

10. Some troublesome pairs are also caused by similarities between suffixes or root endings which sound like suffixes. Repeat the above procedure with these words:

bridle	Briton	capitol	censure	dual
foreword	formerly	ingenious	mantel	moral
populace		principle		stationary

32

11. Still another class is created because of slight changes in sound to indicate different parts of speech. We give some common words from this group below; write in the near-homonym which is related in meaning, being sure that you know which meaning goes with which word:

advice   safe   breath   devise   latter   prophecy   wreath

_____

12. Other words, completely unrelated in meaning, are separated by similar slight differences in sound, and so become troublesome. Write below each of the following words a near-homonym with which it is frequently confused, making sure *you* know the meanings and spellings well enough not to confuse them yourself:

dessert   lightening   loose   tittle

_____

13. Others are just plain "demons" and involve more than one of the above classifications—or defy classification altogether. Treat the following words as you did those in the preceding exercises; where you should indicate more than one homonym or near-homonym, we have shown the number in parentheses:

its   forth   horde   isle (2)   whether

_____

_____

cite (2)   corps (2)   right (3)   their (2)   through (2)   to (2)

_____

_____

_____

4

Suggestions for Using This Book

In this final section of preliminary material, we wish not only to give you some final directions, but also to point out a few ways, beyond the scope of this book, in which the speller may help himself. One of these is by understanding the cause of his poor spelling, and the other is by knowing a specific method for dealing with the "demons," the words not properly taken care of by the generalizations in this book. In discussing first the causes of bad spelling, one fact should be emphasized: there is no one cause of bad spelling. A poor speller may be created by any one of a number of causes, or by a combination of two or more.

Some of the causes are physiological, and should be attended to by the proper kind of doctor before the work outlined here can become effective. Partial or total deafness of either one or both ears can obviously upset the patient's spelling, and if he continues to hear words incorrectly, no amount of study of phonetics is going to make him a good speller. On the other hand, once the deafness is alleviated, he should not expect to become a better speller without some effort and study of the type suggested here.

Similarly, difficulties of vision must be cleared away. Simple nearsightedness or far-sightedness rarely causes trouble in spelling or reading, but when you have your eyes examined, you should ask your ophthalmologist to test your eyes for difficulties in fusion, focusing, and astigmatism. The medical profession itself is not entirely agreed as to how much these latter difficulties affect one's reading and spelling, but there seems to be good evidence that in some cases they do. And obviously, a person who does not see a word distinctly will have a hard time remembering how it looks.

Other physiological causes trouble only the rare cases. Anything, however, which is a drain on your system may affect your spelling—migraine headaches are one of the commonest. What is known as a psychopathic bad speller—one whose bad spelling is caused by some psychological maladjustment—is very rare; much more common are the maladjustments caused by the frustration and sense of failure resulting from not spelling well.

One of the commonest types of spelling error has never been adequately explained; it is the occurrence of reversals in spelling, that is, the writing of *saw* for *was,* of *-de* for *-ed,* and the transposing, reversing, or inverting of any letters. All children do a certain amount of it when they are learning to read and write, but most of them soon outgrow it, so that most adults reverse only occasionally when writing in haste. A small percentage, however, never overcome the tendency, and a good 20 per cent or more of their spelling errors are reversals. The most generally accepted explanation is the hypothesis of "lack of cerebral dominance," which might equally well have been named "uncertain sidedness." The centers in the brain which control all the language functions are in the half of the brain which controls a person's favored side—the left hemisphere in a person who is right-footed, right-handed, and right-eyed, the right hemisphere in a person who prefers the left side. This preference for one side, or dominance, is never properly developed in some people, according to the hypothesis, either because they have an inheritance of both left- and right-sided ancestors, or because, as natural left-handers, they have been forced to be right-handed.

This condition may affect one's linguistic abilities only mildly, or very severely; in speech (stuttering), or in reading, or in spelling, or in all of them; it has no effect whatever on one's intelligence. Those who are at all seriously afflicted with this condition will probably find this book of little help, but will need to turn to an individual tutor.

By all odds the largest group of poor spellers among adults is created by the way they were taught to read in the early grades of elementary school. The method variously known as the "recognition" or "whole-word" or "look-and-say" method emphasizes the entire word, the recognition of it as a unit, much as one might recognize a hieroglyphic. For a few of the better students this meant increased speed in reading. But for most of them it meant disaster in spelling. Little or no attention was paid to individual letters, or to syllables, and the student never learned any method for dealing with unfamiliar words, either in reading or in spelling. Fortunately, although this is the largest group, it is the one that responds most readily to the type of training being offered here.

As we shall be discussing with you primarily those words which can be studied as groups, because some sort of generalization applies to them, we want here to introduce you to a method for attacking words which must be studied individually, the demons which are exceptions to the generalizations. You may also find this a good method to use on words which you have already misspelled in papers, letters, reports, and so on—first analyzing each word to see whether the point at which you made your error is not covered by one of the generalizations which we will shortly study.

Most good spellers depend upon one of three of their senses to tell whether the word is right or not. Most of them will tell you that the word *looks* right. Their memory is predominantly visual. I have known a few people who had to spell the word aloud (i.e. *hear* it spelled) to be sure of the spelling. Their memory is predominantly auditory. And I have read of people who told by the *feel* of the act of writing that the word was correct. Their memory is predominantly kinesthetic. Our method (not original) tries to combine all three senses into one operation, for no matter which sense seems to be most effective, they all help to reinforce one another.

With this method you begin with the word you are studying spelled correctly in front of you—in the dictionary or a book, or your own longhand copy which you are sure is correct. Look at it carefully, breaking it down into syllables if it has more than one (this part is visual). When you think you have looked at the word long enough to get a good mental image of it, cover the example and write the word at the top of a strip of paper three inches wide (this is kinesthetic reinforcement—try to sense how it *feels* to write the word). As you write each letter, spell the word *aloud* (this is auditory reinforcement). Then compare what you have written with the original. If what you wrote is correct, it is probably safe for you to proceed to another word; if you made a mistake, study what your error was, and your original example as a whole once more. Then fold under the top of your strip of paper, covering your first attempt, cover your model, and spell aloud and write the word again. Then compare again. Do this until you have written it correctly five times in a row, comparing after each writing, of course, as it would be unfortunate to impress the wrong motion upon one's kinesthetic memory, or the wrong sounds upon one's auditory memory.

The one type of error which this method will not correct is the one you knew better than to make—but made just the same! You were not thinking about what you were doing when you wrote down the word. Your list of misspelled words is probably full of such mistakes; inability to concentrate on spelling seems to be one of the poor speller's most universal characteristics. His usual explanation is that he was thinking ahead, that his mind "got ahead of his pen." If you feel that this explanation is valid in your case, especially when you are writing under pressure, as on an examination, you might try slowing down a bit and formulating your sentences *in their entirety* before you write a word of each one. Once you have composed your sentence, you can concentrate on the writing (and spelling) of it. Then pause for the next sentence, and so on. You may write shorter answers to your questions, but you may also write answers so much better in quality that your grades will be better. Try this system until our course of study has had a chance to take effect and you can, perhaps, write more rapidly without spelling badly. If you complete our course of study we hope you will be more self-conscious about your spelling, better able to concentrate on what you are doing *and* on what you ought to be doing when you write each word.

With this preliminary material well in your mind, you are about ready to begin work on the phonetic generalizations which form the vital part of this book. The sequence in which we take up the 34 phonemes of English and some of their combinations will be dictated not by the frequency with which they occur in English, or by the amount of trouble they create for spellers, but by their usefulness in teaching you how to make generalizations. Because we believe that you will remember the generalizations better and use them more readily if you discover them yourself, we plan to be as inductive in our method as possible. We will give you wordlists, but not to memorize; they will provide all the evidence you will need for making your generalizations. Follow the directions in the exercises, observe the words carefully, and you should be able to generalize soundly.

This is not an ordinary workbook; it is, rather, a textbook, part of which you are going to write yourself. Writing in the answers to the exercises will add material to your textbook, not the least important being the generalizations you will formulate in some of the exercises. You may, if you wish, add words to the wordlists; having to decide which column is the right one for each example which you add will make you use the generalizations you have formed, and thus help you to use them subconsciously because they have become so familiar to you. The more you add to this book, the more valuable a reference work and companion to your dictionary it will become.

Although we want to be as inductive as possible, there are a few basic principles of spelling for which we must ask you to take our word at first. These are generalizations based on the generalizations you will make; as you go along you will begin to see their validity:

1. One-syllable words do not always behave like multisyllabic ones. One of the most striking examples of this is the way in which several consonant sounds are represented by special phonograms (letters or groups of letters) when they occur at the end of one-syllable words and follow a short vowel. Our next lesson will deal with this; /č/ may not cause you much trouble in spelling—we begin with it, as we suggested above, because it introduces you very nicely to a type of generalization which you will have to make several times.

2. The position of a sound in its syllable—beginning, middle, or end—may influence its spelling. This plays a part, of course, in the illustration just given, but is very important elsewhere too, especially with the vowels.

3. The sound immediately preceding or immediately following the sound under consideration may influence its spelling. Whether a phoneme follows a consonant or a vowel may be important, the most familiar example perhaps being the formation of the plurals of nouns ending in *-y*. And frequently, particularly in unaccented syllables, the pronunciation of a consonant may be altered by the following vowel, as we shall see in the next lesson.

36

4. The national origin of a word may influence its spelling. This fact, of course, is part of the explanation of why our English sound system seems to correspond so badly to our alphabet. Nobody expects you to remember the etymology of every word you encounter (although it is probably true that many of the best spellers are also persons interested in words and their histories), but you should learn to identify the probable origin of large groups of words—Greek for scientific terms, and so on.

Other generalizations will be introduced later as you need them. You are now ready to begin the exercises. Students who have used this book before you have experienced more trouble as a result of not reading the directions carefully enough than through not being able to make the generalizations. Go slowly, read carefully, do as you are directed, and you should be highly successful.

Exercises

1. Compare the list of words you have misspelled with the list of one hundred words most commonly misspelled by college freshmen (see pp. 178–80); study with the method we have suggested any words which appear on both lists.

2. For further practice with this new method, we have listed below some exceptions to generalizations which you will soon make, a few plain demons, and a few commonly misspelled words that should not be misspelled:

cartridge	plaid	yacht	occurred
picture	numerous	majestic	porridge
equipped	handsome	khaki	enough

3. The reversals hardest to catch in proofreading are those which make good words—but not the words you wanted to use. Below are some frequently confused pairs to study:

quite	felt	tried	angel	trial	diary	sacred
quiet	left	tired	angle	trail	dairy	scared

5

We will begin our study of phonic generalizations with the sound /č/, as in *church* or *chitchat*. Below are some examples of words with this sound, and from them you will see that it is one of the sounds in English which is usually represented by a digraph, *ch,* or a trigraph, *tch,* not by a single letter. As there are two possible phonograms for the sound, we need a phonic generalization to guide us in making our choice. If you will do the exercises in this lesson, keeping in mind the generalizations we gave you in the preceding chapter, and observing the following wordlists closely, you will discover when to use *ch* and when *tch.*

Exercises

1	2	3	4	5	6
charm	branch	attach	catch	beach	
cheek	bench	detach	fetch	leech	
children	inch	ostrich	pitch	couch	
chop	scorch	sandwich	notch	brooch	
churl	lurch		crutch	coach	
choose	lynch				
chubby	filch				
	gulch				
	parch				
	squelch				
	staunch				

1. In the spaces provided, write in your answers to the following questions:
   a. Look in your dictionary for words beginning with *tch;* what do you find? (Proper names defy all rules of spelling, so we are not concerned here with them.)

_____

_____

   b. What is suggested to you by the wordlists above as to the usual position of *tch* in a word?

_____

   c. In column 2 what *type* of sound does /č/ follow?

_____

d. In column 5 what type of sound does /č/ follow?

_____

e. In column 4 what type of sound does /č/ follow?

_____

f. What is the difference between the words in column 3 and the words in column 4?

_____

_____

g. Can you now formulate a generalization as to when to use *tch* to represent /č/? Write it below:

_____

_____

2. Write on a piece of scratch paper as many words as you can think of which rhyme with the words given in column 4 (you can start by substituting all the other consonants in the alphabet for the first letter in each word, to see if it makes a word). Any exceptions to your above generalization should be marked with an asterisk or encircled; if you find more than six exceptions, there is probably something wrong with your generalization! Exceptions which you can already spell, write in column 6; the column to the extreme right in the wordlists is always reserved for exceptions after you learn them. If your dictionary has a "Vocabulary of Rhymes," you will find it a help; the rhyming words you want will all be listed under *-atch, -etch, -itch, -otch, -utch*. Now put down all the rhymes you can for these six words:

batch   ketch   ditch   botch   crutch   butch

_____

_____

3. What may appear to you to be exceptions to your generalization about one-syllable words are the result of adding prefixes or suffixes to them, or of compounding them with other words. The generalizations you will make will be for what are called "roots," as opposed to prefixes and suffixes. A few examples of apparently irregular, but actually perfectly regular, words are given below. Add a few of each type:

bewitch   catching   watchdog

_____

_____

_____

4. What you may wish to include as real exceptions, though in some cases they belong in the lists in exercise 3, are words with affixes (usually suffixes) whose roots no longer exist in English as separate words. The suffix *-et*, for example, occurs in diminutives derived from French, as in the word *hatchet*. Sometimes the word to which this or similar suffixes are added no longer exist in English

with a meaning recognizable to most people, as in the word *satchel*. A true exception seems to be the word *kitchen,* descended from the Old English *cycene.* Can you add any words similar to these three to your list of exceptions? Write them below, and in column 6 when you have mastered them:

_____

_____

_____

_____

5. In some parts of the United States the words listed below also sound as though they had a /č/ sound. Pronounce them easily and naturally to yourself, in a sentence if possible; do you hear /č/ anywhere? If you do, you should beware of these words. The /č/ here is the result of the palatalization of the /t/; the /t/ sound is made in the front of the mouth, the /u/ in the back. Some speakers tend to start reshaping their mouths for the /u/ before they have quite finished the /t/, and the result is a /č/ sound. Study the words below, underline the one you think might be most commonly misspelled, and explain why you think so:

aperture	century	furniture	future
nature	picture	temperature	virtue

_____

_____

6. Another type of palatalization occurs in the speech of many Americans when /t/ is followed by /ə/ with an intervening /i/ serving as a glide. The usual result is /š/ as in *action,* but when the *ti* follows an *s* the result is, for many people, /č/ as in *bastion* and *fustian.* Add below any other examples of this which you can find (if your dictionary has a "Vocabulary of Rhymes," look up the entries *-ast, -aust, -est, -ist, -ost, -ust,* and see how many of the words listed there can make new words with *-ian* or *-ion* added at the end):

_____

_____

_____

_____

7. a. Where in your dictionary will you find the rule for forming the plural of words ending in /č/?

_____

b. Write out the rule here for future reference:

_____

_____

Part of this lesson exactly parallels the material of the last lesson, so we will begin with it. As the letter *j* can never end a word in English, but the sound /ǰ/ frequently does, you have a choice between a digraph, *ge,* and a trigraph, *dge,* at the end of the word, just as you did with /č/. With that much of a hint, go ahead and do the first six exercises in this chapter—they will seem familiar to you, and ought to be easy.

At other positions in a word the situation is not so easy as it was with /č/, where there was only one possibility, for /ǰ/ can be represented by *j,* and by *g* before *e, i,* and *y.* As the *e* and *i* after the *g* are sometimes pronounced and sometimes not, the result is that /ǰ/ may be represented by *j, g, ge,* and *gi,* as well as *dge.* The letter *y,* so far as I have been able to discover, is always pronounced after *g.*

There are two groups of words which will cause you the most trouble, so far as /ǰ/ is concerned. One is the group where /ǰ/ is the first sound in the word; *j,* of course, always appears before *a, o,* and *u,* but before *e, i,* and *y, j* and *g* have not divided up the territory at all well, and as a result there is no good generalization to guide you. We may have to let you down like this occasionally, for which we are very sorry. Secondly, you may find troublesome the words which use *ge* or *gi* in the body of the word, as in *advantageous* or *religion,* where it is easy to overlook the *e* or *i.* The remaining exercises in the lesson will give you a few guides for spelling /ǰ/ in the body of the word.

Exercises

1	2	3	4	5	6
jaundice	change	college	badge	cage	
jelly	merge	privilege	hedge	gouge	
gem	singe	marriage	bridge	huge	
jig	bulge	foliage	dodge	page	
ginger	scourge	sacrilege	judge	rage	
jog	lunge	forage	pledge	siege	
jug	large	allege	ridge	stooge	
gypsy	bilge		lodge		
gentle			nudge		
jest					
gin					
jilt					

(continued)

1	2	3	4	5	6
engine					
reject					
abject					
digest					
diligent					
religion					
imagine					
subject					
courageous					
energy					

1. In the spaces provided, write in the answers to the following questions:

   a. Look in your dictionary for words beginning with *dge;* what do you find?

   _____

   b. What is suggested to you by the wordlists above as to the usual position of *dge* in a word?

   _____

   c. In column 2 what *type* of sound does /ǰ/ follow?

   _____

   d. In column 5 what type of sound does /ǰ/ follow?

   _____

   e. In column 4 what type of sound does /ǰ/ follow?

   _____

   f. What is the difference between the words in column 3 and the words in column 4?

   _____

   g. Can you now formulate a generalization as to when to use *dge* to represent /ǰ/? Write it below:

   _____

   _____

2. Write on a piece of scratch paper as many words as you can think of which rhyme with the words given. Any exceptions to your generalization in exercise 1 should be marked with an asterisk or encircled; if you find more than five or six exceptions, there is probably something wrong with your generalization! Exceptions which you can already spell, write in column 6. If your dictionary has a "Vocabulary of Rhymes," you will find it a help; the rhyming words you want will all be listed under *-adge, -edge, -idge, -odge, -udge.* Now put down all the rhymes you can for these five words, both one-syllable and multi-syllabic rhymes:

badge	dredge	bridge	dodge	fudge

_____

_____

3. We would remind you that what may appear at first glance to be exceptions to the generalization which you have just made may actually be only regular one-syllable words either compounded or with an affix added. We give some examples below; add to them others which you think might cause you trouble:

adjudge	dodger	bridgework

_____

_____

_____

_____

4. What you may wish to include as real exceptions, though in some cases they belong in your lists in exercise 3, are words with affixes whose root no longer exists in English by itself or is at best rarely used. The French diminutive suffix -_et_ again provides us with an example in the word _budget_ (originally, a little leather bag), which seems to have little to do with the verb, _budge,_ to move. Somewhat more remote is the group of words ending in -_eon,_ many of which seem to be derived ultimately from the Latin suffix -_ion_ (if you can, look up in the _Oxford English Dictionary_ the derivation of _gudgeon, pigeon,_ and _widgeon_). A real exception is the word _cudgel,_ in which the -_el_ is not derived from the old French diminutive suffix, but was part of the word for as far back as we can trace it in Anglo-Saxon. See now if you can add any other words of the type of these examples; write them below, and in column 6 when you have mastered them:

_____

_____

_____

_____

5. In some parts of the United States the words listed below also sound as though they had a /ǰ/ sound. Pronounce them easily and naturally to yourself, in a sentence if possible; do you hear /ǰ/ anywhere? If you do, you should be careful with these words. The /ǰ/ here is the result of the palatalization of the /d/; when the following /u/ is unaccented, some speakers tend to start reshaping their mouths for the /u/ before they have quite finished with the /d/, and the result is a /ǰ/ sound. This phenomenon does not occur as frequently as the corresponding one for /č/, but see if you can add any further examples to the three given below:

verdure	graduate	individual

_____

_____

_____

6. The palatalization of /d/ before /ə/ with an /i/ glide intervening is not as widespread or as stable as that of /t/; about the only word in which /ǰ/ is heard for *di* in almost every dialect in America is *soldier*. A few others, such as *guardian* and *invidious,* acquire a /ǰ/ in some dialects, but not universally. As a guide to yourself, write in below any other words in your speech in which you notice a /ǰ/ which is represented by *di* in spelling:

_____

_____

7. a. Where in your dictionary will you find the rule for dropping final *e* before suffixes?

_____

b. What is the general rule? Write it out here for future use:

_____

c. Did you discover a special rule for words ending in *-ge?* You should have. Write it out here:

_____

_____

d. Did you find a special rule applying only to words ending in *-dge?* You should have. Write it out here too:

_____

_____

8. Look at the words in the second half of column 1. Assuming, as you may, that this brief list is representative, you should be able to make some observation as to when you will find *j* in the body of a word before *e, i,* or *y.* Formulate your generalization here:

_____

_____

9. The only "trouble spots" in the body of the word, therefore, are those places where /ǰ/ is represented by *ge* or *gi,* especially before /æ/, /a/, /u/, or /ə/, where you would expect *j.* Inspect the following words and see if you can arrive at a generalization as to when you are most likely to encounter these digraphs. Write your generalization below the words:

courageous	advantageous	religious	gorgeous
religion	manageable	changeable	sergeant

_____

_____

10. Look in your dictionary for words beginning with *jy-;* what you find true of the beginnings of words is true of every position in a word. What then is your generalization? Write it below:

_____

_____

11. Look up in your dictionary the pronunciation of *oleomargarine;* how do you pronounce the *g?* Should this word go in your column of exceptions?

_____

_____

_____

/b/, /g/, /p/

For the first two or three weeks we shall let you relax every third lesson, and work on the sounds which are most consistent in their representation. Some words, of course, are "phonetic for spelling but not for reading," and vice versa. The sound /g/, for example, is quite regular, being generally represented by *g*, and so is little trouble to spellers; but *g* does not always represent /g/, having usurped some of *j*'s work, and consequently not all words with *g* are phonetic for the reader.

The three sounds for today's lesson, /b/, /g/, and /p/, are generally consistent in the way in which they are represented. They and all the other regular consonants present difficulties only when they are doubled, or when the sound has disappeared from the pronunciation and the letter remains.

One large group of double letters is created by the addition of prefixes and suffixes, as we have seen. Further, during the Old English Period, these aspirated stops (particularly the voiceless ones) were frequently doubled before /l/ and /r/, as in *apple, cripple, pepper, bitter,* and *utter.* Unfortunately in both this and the later doubling of consonants to indicate vowel length many words were overlooked. Consequently the most troublesome but fortunately least numerous of all are the double letters in the roots of words. These are particularly bad because in normal speech only one sound is made for the two letters —that is, *rabbit* and *habit* rhyme perfectly.

Many of the silent letters in the language occur as the silent partners in pairs of consonants both of which at one time were pronounced together in the same syllable as a blend. The exercises will introduce you to these fossil blends, and show you something about the peculiarities of their behavior. Occasionally, we may add a note about the history of the silent letter when it seems interesting; but do the exercise before reading the note.

You may wish to use the two columns we have provided for each of these regular sounds to build your own wordlists as you master the words. Don't waste space with words which are easy; words like *bag* and *gap* and *beg* should not present any problems, though *gapping* and *begging* and *beggar* might. We suggest, therefore, that in one column you put words which raise the question of whether to double the letter or not (both *rabbit* and *habit* would be suitable for /b/); in the second put words involving silent letters.

Exercises

1	2	3	4	5	6
rabbit habit	lamb	begging beggar begin	sign	gapping gaping	ptomaine

1. Look up the pronunciation of the following words in your dictionary and try to figure out a generalization to explain when the *b* is silent after /m/. (This weakening of /b/ occurred in the sixteenth century.) We've given you a hint above, but see if you can figure out the generalization without looking back:

bomb	catacomb	climbing	comber	cumbersome
limb	lumber	lamb	limber	mumble
number	plumber	succumb	timber	tomb

Write your generalization here:

_____

_____

_____

_____

2. Look up the pronunciations and etymologies of the following words (go to the *Oxford English Dictionary* if you can), and see if you can arrive at a phonic generalization as to when *b* is silent before /t/:

debt	doubt	subtle	subtract	subterfuge

Write your generalization here:

_____

_____

_____

_____

NOTE: In a very few English words the *b* has not grown silent—it has never been pronounced at all. The words in this small group were borrowed from French without any *b* at some time during the Middle Ages (*debt* and *doubt* appear, for example, as *dette* and *doute* in Chaucer's works in the fourteenth century). But during the sixteenth century Renaissance in England, admiration for the Latin language reached such a high point that pedants who observed that *dette* was derived from the Latin *debitus* insisted that the *b* be restored to the spelling—and there the *b* is today, in *debt* and *doubt* and a few other words, without ever having been an official part of the pronunciation of those words! The *p* in *receipt* has a similar history also.

3. Look up the pronunciation of the following words in your dictionary, and try to draw a conclusion about the sounding of *g* before /n/. This was a weakening of /g/ which occurred in the seventeenth century. Write your generalization below the words:

agnostic	design	dignity	feign
gnaw	ignominious	sign	ignorant
impugn	malign	reign	gnome

_____

_____

_____

4. Do likewise with *g* before /m/:

    diaphragm   paradigm   phlegm

_____

_____

5. Look up in your dictionary all the words beginning with *pn, ps,* and *pt.* List below the prefixes or combining forms which you think would be most helpful for you to remember (because you know some of the words containing them). Give also the *meaning* of the root or prefix. What type of word, in general, employs these three combinations of letters? Write your answers to *all* these questions below:

_____

_____

_____

_____

_____

6. Do you remember why the *p* is silent in these words? Make a note in the margin here of the page references which explained why, and see if you can discover any other examples of the same phenomena:

    cupboard   clapboard   raspberry

_____

_____

7. /g/ can, of course, appear before *e, i,* and *y.* To allow it to do so English employs two devices: (1) it represents /g/ by *gu* as in *guess* and *guilt;* and (2) it doubles the *g* as in *nugget, noggin,* and *piggy.* This means that ordinarily /g/ does not precede /ĭ/ in a word in English. Often, of course, *g* represents /g/ before *e, i,* and *y* without recourse to these devices, and at times these devices are used where they are not needed, as in *guard.* Among the following words are several that are exceptional; underline the exceptions:

begin	beggar	suggest	bigger	regard
guest	digest	guitar	bogus	bogey

8

/æ/, /a/, /ɔ/, /o/

In this lesson we plan to take up four of the simple vowels which are closely related in ordinary speech. The three sounds commonly represented by *o*, /a/, /ɔ/, and /o/, occur in the speech of most Americans, though to varying extents and in differing relationships. For many of us the two sounds /a/ and /ɔ/ are complementary, and we are not ordinarily conscious of shifting from one to the other. That is, in many words the two sounds are allophones and not distinct phonemes which distinguish "what is said from what might have been said." For many Americans /o/ occurs only in the word *gonna,* and even for those who use the sound more extensively, it is still an allophone of the sounds represented by *o*.

There are, also, about 150 words in everyday use of which the pronunciation varies from /æ/ to /a/ from dialect to dialect.[1] For example, *bath* may be pronounced /bæð/ or /ba ð/, *glass* may be pronounced /glæs/ or /glas/. In some individuals this vowel sound is prolonged until it becomes a complex vowel nucleus, /baHð/ or /glaHs/, but we must discuss it later. In another sizable group of words the sound /æ/ is changed to /ɔ/ by a neighboring sound. An analogous process can be seen at work in Early Modern English, when such words as *hale* /heyl/ became *haul* /hoHl/, and Old English *æl* /æl/ became *awl* /oHl/. In these older changes the spelling has become *au* or *aw,* and as the syllable was usually accented, the sound has generally been lengthened from the simple /ɔ/ to the vowel nucleus /oH/. My ears are not sharp enough, frankly, to hear the distinction between the simple and complex vowels clearly, except that the latter is held longer (cf. *law* with *authority*). I can feel a difference when I use them, however; the point at which the sound is made in my mouth remains constant for the simple vowel, whereas for the nucleus I can feel that point rising toward the top of my mouth.

Some of the differences between British and American pronunciation involve the vowels we are studying today. For example, /æ/ is not nearly so common a sound in England as in America, although it varies in use from one part of the island to another. On the other hand the British use /o/ much more than we do; they differentiate the /a/ in *father* from an /o/ in *fodder,* for example, a distinction limited to parts of New England and the Southeast in America.

In the wordlists we have given you examples of these different variations in sound, and when they are most likely to occur. The exercises will give you a chance to sort them out. The vowels, whether simple or complex, are the part of any word which varies most in pronunciation from dialect to dialect, and consequently are the sounds hardest to deal with in a spelling book of this sort. But in general most people, we believe, pronounce the words in column 1 with an /æ/ sound. If your pronunciation of the *a* in the next two columns is different, you will find the generalizations helpful.

---

[1] H. L. Mencken, *The American Language,* 4th edition, New York, Knopf, 1936, p. 334.

Exercises

1	2	3	4	5	6
add	water	all	cork	odd	plaid
pat	want	alter	scorn	pot	
battle	wash	already	border	bottle	
gabble	swamp	ball	forest	gobble	
jabber	swan	scald	orange	jobber	
that	squalid	malt	moral	fodder	
		caldron	torment		
			horrible		
			correspond	father	
			porcupine	bar	
				hard	
				part	
			frog		
			log		
		rebuttal	mock		
		refusal	knock		
		interval			
			honk		
			gone		
			gong		
			long		
		alchemy	broth		
		alcohol	cloth		
		alcove			
			off		
			office		
			coffee		
			soft		
			often		
			toss		
			moss		
			lacrosse		
			cost		

1. For many people the sound represented by *a* in column 1 is not the same as that represented by *a* in column 2. If you are one of them, answer the following questions:

    a. Is the sound represented by *a* in column 2 /æ/ or /ɔ/?

b. Under what circumstances do you think this change of pronunciation seen in column 2 occurs? (Remember that *qu* represents /kw/ most of the time.)

_____

2. For many people the sound represented by *a* in column 1 is not the same as that represented by *a* in column 3. If you are one of them, answer these questions:

a. Is the sound represented by *a* in the first part of column 3 /æ/ or /ɔ/?

_____

b. Under what circumstances do you think this change in pronunciation occurs?

_____

c. Look up the suffix *-al* in your dictionary; what is its usual pronunciation? All words ending in an unaccented *-al* are pronounced the same way, and form one group of exceptions to your generalization in b., above. The second group of words in column 3 provides you with some illustrations.

_____

d. Look up the etymology of the words in the third group in column 3. From what language do they all originally come? They represent another group of exceptions to your generalization in b., which should certainly have had the word "frequently" in it rather than "always."

_____

e. What is the combining form of *all* at the beginning of words? List below as many words containing it as you can find in your dictionary:

_____

_____

3. Many people hear an /ɔ/ in the words in column 4; whether you do or not, or how extensively you do, will depend upon the dialect you speak and the sound following the *o*. Although this pronunciation causes little or no trouble in spelling, you may find it useful and interesting to answer the following questions:

a. Before what sounds do *you* use an /ɔ/?

_____

b. We all have exceptional words; I, for example, pronounce *most* with a /ow/, not rhyming with *cost* at all. Such words you should record here or in the column of exceptions for your own guidance.

_____

_____

_____

_____

4. This exercise is concerned with the distinction we referred to on p. 49 between British and American speech. In words in which /a/ is represented by *a,* the two are close enough so that a man untrained in linguistic listening cannot tell the difference. But in the much larger group in which Americans pronounce the *o* as /a/ in most dialects, the British use /o/. Answering the following questions may help you:

   a. In column 5, do you pronounce the *o* in the first group of words as you do the *a* in the second group?

   _____

   b. If your answer was No, can you think of any words which are spelled with an *a* but which you pronounce like the words in the first group, or any words spelled with an *o* but which you pronounce like the second group? List them below:

   _____

   _____

   c. Do you pronounce either or both of the vowels in column 5 like the *a* in the last three words in column 2?

   _____

   d. The second part of column 5 is far from complete but quite representative; after inspecting it and the second half of column 2, when would you say you would be most likely to encounter *a* representing /a/?

   _____

NOTE: We must anticipate a little here, and warn you that one of the most troublesome parts of dealing with the simple vowels is that when they occur in unaccented syllables (particularly when they stand alone, but at other times too) they tend to become leveled and all sound alike. This common sound is generally represented by the phonetic symbol /ə/, so that we will discuss this problem further when we get there. Meanwhile here are some examples of syllables with *a* and *o* in them in unaccented syllables:

a	*o*
miracle	mythology
pyramid	halcyon
sycamore	symphony
drama	daffodil
tenant	random
vigilance	glutton

Today we take up the one of the four generalizations listed in Chapter 4 which we have not yet encountered, namely, that the national origin of a word may influence its spelling. The richness of vocabulary of English is attributable in no small part to its extensive borrowings from foreign languages—a debt which English continues to acknowledge every day in some of its less common methods of spelling certain sounds.

Exercises

1	2	3	4	5	6
sheriff	dwarf	waif	staff	graph	laugh
plaintiff	golf	brief	eff	neophyte	cough
tariff	wharf	loaf	cliff	phonics	enough
bailiff		proof	doff	sulphur	rough
distaff			buff	alphabet	tough
				paragraph	trough
differ		safe			
duffel		life			
suffer					
taffeta					

1. In the spaces provided, write the answers to the following questions, based on the above word-lists, ignoring columns 5 and 6 for the moment:

   a. What seems to be the usual way to represent /f/ at the end of a word following a consonant?

   _____

   b. What seem to be the usual ways to represent /f/ at the end of a word following a long vowel?

   _____

   c. What seems to be the usual way to represent /f/ at the end of a word following a short vowel?

   _____

   d. Look at column 1 and see if you can write down two ways in which this last generalization differs from those you have made before for *tch* and *dge:*

   (1) _____

   (2) _____

2. Write as before on a piece of scratch paper as many words as you can think of which rhyme with those listed below. Any exceptions to your generalization in question 1c. should go into column 6 when you have mastered them. (Your dictionary's "Vocabulary of Rhymes," if it has one, will save you time on this exercise).

staff	eff	cliff	doff	buff

_____

_____

_____

3. Write down as many words as you can think of, both one syllable and multisyllabic, which rhyme with those listed below. From the results, can you make any generalizations as to how to spell /f/ after a long vowel at the end of a word? If so, write them in below your rhyming words:

safe	brief	life	loaf	proof

_____

_____

_____

_____

4. Look up the etymologies of the words in column 5, and then answer the following questions:

a. Do the words all have a common ultimate origin?

_____

b. What language is it?

_____

c. Can you make a generalization as to when *ph* is used to represent /f/? Write it below, and check it by looking up some other words you know which employ *ph:*

_____

d. In what areas of learning do you expect to find words which use *ph* to represent /f/?

_____

5. In the sixth column are six words in which /f/ is represented by *gh;* this is one of the most unstable combinations in the English language, and it is hard to be inductive about it. Can you use these six words in *one* sentence? Such a sentence might help you remember these words. Write it in below. Then look up in your "Vocabulary of Rhymes," if your dictionary has one, the other words in which *gh* represents /f/. These words are not nearly so common or useful as the six we have listed, but if any are part of your vocabulary, try to incorporate them into your sentence:

_____

_____

_____

6. The double letter, *ff*, in the middle of a word (see the second part of column 1) occurs, of course, only after a short vowel. The converse, that /f/ after a short vowel will always be represented by *ff*, is distinctly *not* true. But even this much information can be helpful. Explain how it can help you with the spelling of these four words, for example:

professor   prefer   rifle   profile

_____

_____

_____

/l/, /m/, /n/

This is almost a review lesson, for many of the words which you will put in your column for words with a double *l* will be one-syllable words ending in /l/ following a short vowel—and the generalization is the same as that which you have just made for similar words ending in /f/, except that with /l/ the generalization does not carry over to multisyllabic words, and there is no complicating special phonogram in words of Greek extraction. /l/ is silent in a number of combinations, some of which are rather curious to anyone interested in language and how it works.

The sounds /m/ and /n/ may be treated together, in part at least, as they combine to form the only blend in which either one is regularly silent. When *mn* is initial, the *m* is silent; when final (much commoner), the *n* is silent.

Exercises

1	2	3	4	5
lull	talk	hammer	manner	mnemonic solemn

1. Underline the words in the following group in which *l* is silent:

talk	elk	milk	yolk	bulk
folk	silk	hulk	walk	skulk

On the basis of this can you formulate a generalization as to when *l* is silent before /k/? Write it out below. This generalization may not be much help in putting the *l* where it belongs; but it ought to be a great help in keeping you from putting in *l*'s where there is no need for one:

_____

_____

2. Underline the words in the following group which do not sound the *l*. Then write in your generalization as to when *l* is silent before /m/:

palm	calm	almanac	elm	qualm	helm
salmon	psalm	almond	almoner	alms	holm†

3. Two more groups involving silent *l* are too small to need a generalization, but can conveniently be learned as groups. Can you think of any to add to them?

could	would	should	calf	half	behalf

4. Underline the words below in which part of *mn* is silent; below the words write in a generalization explaining when *m* is silent, when *n* is silent, and when both are pronounced:

condemn	column	hymn	limn	mnemonic
autumnal	damning	indemnify	solemnity	

† Look this one up and decide how much you will use it before cluttering up your generalization with it.

/k/

Although the letter *k* is not too common in English, the sound /k/ is very common, and rather troublesome because it can be represented in so many different ways: by *k*, of course, and also by *c*, *ck*, *ch*, *qu*, *que*, and even *kh*. The generalizations involved, however, are merely new applications of familiar principles, so we may proceed at once to our wordlists and exercises. (The special combination /ks/ we will discuss later, in Chapter 14.)

Exercises

1	2	3	4	5	6	7
critic	bank	take	black	Christmas	clique	khaki
phonic	elk	eke	deck	chorus	unique	
almanac	risk	like	kick	chaos	opaque	
awoke	cork	joke	flock	stomach	plaque	
mistake	bulk	fluke	struck	catechism	grotesque	
rebuke				school	bisque	
				ache		
		steak			conquer	
		cheek			coquet	
		shriek			liquor	
		spook			tourniquet	
		soak			piquant	

1. On the basis of generalizations you have made before, you should be able, after inspecting the first four columns above, to make another generalization governing the use of *ck* to represent /k/. Write it below:

_____

_____

2. Other than *ck*, what symbols are commonly used at the end of one-syllable words to represent /k/, and *when?* Forget about columns 5 and 6 in the wordlists for the moment.

_____

3. The regular group of irregularities appears with *ck* as with *tch* and *dge:* the phonogram appears in the middle of the word before a small group of obscure or apparent suffixes, of which *-le* (or *-el*) and *-et* are the commonest. How many other examples can you discover by looking for rhymes with the examples given? Write your examples in:

shackle	freckle	sickle	cockle	buckle	chicken

_____

_____

_____

_____

jacket		cricket	docket	bucket	beckon

_____

_____

_____

_____

4. Look up the etymologies of all the words in group 1 in column 6; what does what you find suggest to you as to the origin of words ending in -*que?* Write your answer below:

_____

_____

5. Look up the etymologies of all the words in column 5; write below your conclusion as to when to use *ch* to represent /k/:

_____

_____

6. Inspect column 1 carefully. What generalizations can you make about how to represent /k/ at the end of multisyllabic words which are not of Greek or French origin? Remember that a final silent *e,* separated from the preceding vowel by a single consonant sound, makes that preceding vowel long. You should be able to make two generalizations; write them here:

(1) _____

(2) _____

7. Look up the etymologies of all the words in your dictionary beginning with *kh.* To what language or group of languages are we indebted for this unusual digraph for /k/? Are there any common words other than *khaki* that begin with it? If so, write them down:

_____

_____

8. Look up in your dictionary the pronunciation of all words beginning with *kn.* What has happened to the *k?* You may want to keep a list of words with this fossil blend which are troublesome:

_____

_____

9. The letters *c* and *k* divide the labor of representing /k/ at the beginning of words quite well (disregarding for now the words in which *ch* may be used). Answer the following questions, and you will see just how they divide the work:

    a. How many pages in your dictionary are devoted to words beginning with *k?*

_____

    b. How many pages of your dictionary are devoted to words beginning with *c* followed by *a, o, u,* or a consonant?

_____

    c. Look at the etymologies of some of the words in your dictionary beginning with *k* followed by *a, o, u,* or a consonant—for example, the following:

kangaroo	kapok	kayak	klieg	kosher
kowtow	kraft	kuchen	kumquat	

    What do these etymologies suggest to you as to the usual type of word in which *k* encroaches on *c*'s domain?

_____

_____

10. Look up the etymologies of all the words in group 2 in column 6; do they suggest anything to you about the origin of words in which *qu* represents /k/? Write your findings below:

_____

Some of these etymologies are rather interesting; *liquor* is another example of what is known as backwriting, which we have observed already in the spelling of *debt* and *doubt.* In the fourteenth century Chaucer spelled the word *licour,* giving it the same spelling as the French word from which it had been borrowed. Later, however, it was recognized that the word was related to the Latin *liquor.* The old spelling was restored, but the French pronunciation was retained.

60

12

One letter in the English alphabet, *c*, has no sound of its own. As we have seen, before *a, o, u*, and the consonants, *c* represents /k/; in this lesson we complete the picture: before *e, i*, and *y*, *c* represents /s/. /s/ too is a very common sound in English, and before *a, o, u*, and the consonants must be represented by *s*, of course. Unfortunately before the other vowels *s* and *c* do not divide the work as neatly as do *k* and *c*, and often the poor speller is left with only the dictionary and his memory to rely upon. This situation is further aggravated by the fact that another fossil blend, *sc*, also can represent /s/ before *e, i*, and *y*. And terminally in a word /s/ may be represented by *ss, ce, se*, and *sce*. In spite of this confusion, however, there are a few useful generalizations which can be made.

Exercises

1	2	3	4	5	6
amass	grace	dance	class	scene	
surpass	fleece	fence	dress	scent	
caress	spice	wince	miss	science	
address	dose	nonce	boss	scion	
dismiss	noose	ounce	fuss	scythe	
emboss		dunce	brass		
discuss			guess		
albatross			loss		
abyss			bliss		
analysis	vase	else		descend	
syllabus	cease	pulse		disciple	
avarice	vise				
prejudice	gross	lapse		coalesce	
	truce	glimpse		convalescent	
		eclipse		adolescence	
apace		copse			
erase		corpse			
release					
advice		sparse			
choice		terse			
grandiose		fierce			
produce		horse			
excuse		course			
		purse			

1. From examining the wordlists, columns 1 through 4, what generalization can you make regarding the spelling of /s/ at the end of one-syllable words following a short vowel?

2. The spelling of /s/ at the end of a word following a consonant depends upon that consonant and the vowel preceding it. Do the following exercises and you may get some help in choosing between -*se* and -*ce* (you will find the generalizations you make much more reliable for one-syllable words than for longer ones):

a. How is a final /s/ spelled after /n/?

_____

b. List below all the *one-syllable* exceptions that you can think of (i.e. words rhyming with the top group in column 3 but not agreeing with your generalization in a.):

_____

_____

c. You will find that some of the words you listed above in b. are also the root of longer words. For example, *tense* is the main root also of *intense* and *pretense*. List below all such families of words that you can think of. Include also groups such as the words built on -*pense*, on a root which is not a word in itself:

_____

_____

_____

_____

d. What is the usual spelling for a final /s/ after /l/ or /p/?

_____

e. What is the usual pronunciation of the inflectional ending -*s* (for plurals of nouns, etc.) following /p/?

_____

f. Disregarding the exceptions covered by your answer to e., list below any exceptions you can think of to your generalization in d. (i.e. words which rhyme with the second and third groups in column 3 but do not agree with your conclusions in d.):

_____

_____

g. What generalizations (you will have to make two) can you make about the spelling of final /s/ after /r/? Write them out below:

(1) _____

(2) _____

62

h. List below words which rhyme with those in column 3, group 4, but which do not follow the generalizations which you made in g.:

_____

_____

_____

3. List below all the one-syllable words you can think of which rhyme with the words in column 4 but do not agree with your generalization in exercise 1. Some of these are very common:

_____

_____

_____

_____

You will notice that at least two of the commonest of these words are shortened forms of longer words.

4. Final /s/ following a long vowel presents difficulties. The only *really* dependable generalizations are that after *oo* you always use -*se,* and after *oi* you use -*ce.* You can discover what appears most frequently after each of the other so-called long vowels by making lists of words rhyming with those in column 2, and in part 2 of column 1:

_____

_____

_____

_____

_____

_____

5. Multisyllabic words ending in /s/ following a short vowel also present problems. By all odds the commonest phonogram is -*ss,* but a look at the first part of column 1 will show you many exceptions. Doing the following exercises will point out some which may be remembered as groups:

a. What is the meaning of the suffix -*mas?* Write it out below, with as many words using it as you know:

_____

_____

b. In some French words and phrases, particularly those recently borrowed, -*sse* takes the place of -*ss* at the end of the word, as in *finesse* and *en masse.* List below any other examples you can think of:

_____

_____

c. What is the meaning of the suffix *-esce?* How many verbs ending with it can you list below?

_____

_____

Related noun and adjective forms end in *-escence* and *-escent,* as in *adolescence* and *adolescent.*

d. List below as many words as you can which, like *analysis* in column 1, end in *-sis.* Look up the etymologies of these words; from what language do they all seem to come, and what type of word most generally uses this ending?

_____

How do you form the plural of these words ending in *-sis?*

_____

e. What is the meaning of the suffix *-ous?* Write it out below. What part of speech is it usually found in?

_____

f. Look up the etymologies of *syllabus* and any other words ending in *-us* that you can think of. From what language do they come? What part of speech do they usually represent? In what level of usage do they occur most frequently? Write your answers below:

_____

_____

g. In what type of word does the phonogram *-ss* appear most commonly?

_____

6. The digraph *sc* should be considered a fossil blend. In Latin it was pronounced /sk/, but usually in Old French, before it ever got to English, it lost the /k/ before /e/, /i/, and /y/. At the end of a word it appears only in the suffix *-esce,* and one or two other rare words. In the middle of a word it will often (not always) appear after a Latin prefix, as in *de·scend.* At the beginning of the word there is as little to guide you as there is in choosing between *s* and *c* before *e, i,* and *y.* Begin a list below of words containing this blend.

_____

_____

13

/d/, /t/, /ed/

We take up today three related sounds, /d/, /t/, and /ed/. Were it not for the inflectional endings of the past tense and past participle, and their annoying way of changing their pronunciation after certain sounds, /d/ and /t/ would be among the most regular of sounds, being always represented by *d* and *t* respectively, and rarely remaining silent. After voiceless sounds (except /t/), however, *-ed* is pronounced /t/ as in *jumped,* and after voiced sounds (except /d/), *-ed* is pronounced /d/ as in *sailed.* After *t* and *d* the suffix is pronounced /ed/. The problem is not a serious one, however, as it occurs only at the end of some words; just stop long enough to think about what you are doing, and realize that you are dealing with a past participle or a past tense. The fact that so many students do make such errors as *equipted* for *equipped* or *drownded* for *drowned* does suggest that they do not always think about what they are doing, and that much student writing is done without benefit of the student's full consciousness.

In order that you may see more specifically what sounds create which pronunciations for *-ed,* we have devoted three columns of our wordlists to *-ed.* There is also one column for each of the double letters, *dd* and *tt;* the few silent letters can all go into the column of exceptions, the blank column to the right.

Exercises

1	2	3	4	5	6
		/d/	/t/	/ed/	
addition	better	played	doffed	corded	
adder	pity	orbed	backed	rented	
radish	ditty	freed	jumped		
bidder		lagged	chased		
consider		spied	dished		
		dodged	arched		
		lulled	taxed		
		farmed			
		burned			
		banged			
		toed			
		jarred			
		clothed			
		mewed			
		lived			
		fizzed			
		garaged			

1. The English language does not particularly like three consonant sounds in a row (remember how few three-sound blends there are), and as a consequence words long established in the language will, in many dialects, drop one of the three consonants (usually, *but not always,* the middle one). Although *d* and *t* are not silent in any fossil blends, this antagonism of the language for three consonant sounds in a row makes them silent in some dialects in a few words. Study the following list and underline the words in which *d* is silent in your speech:

handkerchief	handicraft	handsome	handwriting
grandfather	Wednesday	grandma	wedlock

2. Similarly, underline any of the following words in which *t* is silent:

chasten	fasten	hasten	listen	poster
soften	castle	mortgage	faster	softly

Can you explain why the *t* is silent before *-en?* (You may want to look back at page 16 for a hint). Write out your answer here:

_____

_____

3. We have given you examples of *-ed* added on to most of the sounds which at all commonly end words in English. A few words, however, such as *dream, learn,* and *spell,* allow the *-ed* to be pronounced as either /d/ or /t/. And another small group, in special meanings and situations, has retained the *-ed* as a separate syllable, as *be·lov·ed* and *learn·ed.* Add any others that you can think of or happen to encounter to the lists below:

/d/ or /t/	/d/ or /ed/
dreamed	beloved
learned	learned
spelled	

_____

_____

_____

_____

66

14

Today we take up a pair of consonant sounds, /ks/. We have to do this because they are sometimes represented by a single letter, *x*, and because they present problems to uncertain spellers. Having just discussed /k/ and /s/, we think this an appropriate time to straighten out the many different combinations which can represent /ks/: for example, *cc* in *accent, cks* in *backs, kes* in *rakes, ks* in *barks, x* in *ax, cs* in *relics, chs* in *monarchs.* This is not all as chaotic as it may seem, however. Several of these combinations occur only when the inflectional ending -*s* is added to a word ending in /k/. If you are only conscious enough to know what you are doing, you won't confuse *tax* with *tacks* or make any other similar error. Much more tricky is the problem presented by a word like *accent.* Many of them, including *accent,* are the result of assimilation, which we explained in the second chapter, but a few, like *flaccid,* do not provide even that much of a clue. When the /ks/ sounds appear between two vowels, the /k/ and /s/ are put in different syllables in pronunciation, even though it is customary in writing to place the *x* with the first vowel, as in *flax·en.* Even pronunciation, therefore, will not be of much help. Do the exercises and use your new method for studying difficult words, and you should come out all right. Remember that the uncertain speller, apparently feeling that the English language and his own vocabulary are in some great conspiracy to make spelling as difficult as possible, invariably chooses the most exotic phonogram available, the least probable alternative. Play the percentages even in spelling!

Exercises

1	2	3	4	5
lax	accent	lacks	aches	cliques
flax	accident	flocks		
mix	occident			
box	succinct			
crux	accept	makes		
annex		likes		
expend		jokes		
laxity				
climax				
perplex		creaks		
prefix		soaks	flaccid	
crucifix				
paradox				
		relics		
		lyrics		
		epochs		
		stomachs		

1. We suggest that in adding words to the lists, you place in column 1 words using *x* to represent /ks/. Words with the prefix *ex-* are too common and too easy, so don't fill up your space with them. As you add words to this list, what do you notice about the representation of /ks/ at the end of a word when the /s/ is *not* the inflectional ending?

_____

_____

2. We suggest that you put in the second column further examples of *cc* to represent /ks/ as a result of assimilation. Examples of *cc* for /ks/ which are not the result of assimilation are much less common, and should be put in column 4—it and column 5 are being reserved for unusual combinations. Underline any of the following words which seem to show signs of assimilation:

     access   succeed   flaccid   accelerate

     occident   eccentric   succinct   vaccine

Look up in your dictionary any words about which you are not sure.

3. We suggest that you put in the third column examples of troublesome words ending in /ks/ when the inflectional /s/ *is* added. The combinations of letters used to represent /ks/ in this column appear only rarely in the middle of a word, and then usually in compound words which ought to cause you no trouble. The first three lists below are begun with compound words; the fourth has one of the unusual words containing an odd combination in the root of the word. See how far you can extend the columns we have begun for you:

     backstop   lakeside   inkstand   tocsin

_____

_____

_____

4. The fourth and fifth columns in the wordlists are for unusual combinations to represent /ks/. As you run across such words, jot them down below, then study them with your new method, and when you have mastered them, write them in in the wordlists. Those to be listed under *cliques* you can be learning as you learn the words for column 6 in Chapter 11.

_____

_____

5. Look up the following in your dictionary: *ac-, ax-, ex-;* did you learn anything that might help you *not* to confuse *accept* and *except* in spelling anymore? Look up the derivations of these two words also.

_____

_____

/z/

The sound /z/ is an appropriate one at this point because it is represented by *s* and *x* as well as by *z*. We will let the wordlists and exercises straighten you out as to how you represent /z/.

Exercises

1	2	3	4	5	6
phrase	jazz	xylophone	criticize	criticism	fez
blaze	fizz	xenophobia	idolize	organism	does
ease	buzz	anxiety	lionize		
breeze					
wise				microcosm	
size					
chose					
doze				paroxysm	
fuse					
noise					
choose					
ooze					
rouse					
browse					
blowze					

   1. In column 2 of our wordlists for /z/ we have given you what may appear to be the evidence for a generalization similar to ones you have already made for /f/, /l/, and /s/. But before you make such a generalization, do the following exercises:

     a. Either using your "Vocabulary of Rhymes" or thinking of as many words as you can ending in /z/ following a short vowel, write those ending in *zz* in column 2 and those ending with some other phonogram in column 6 of the wordlists.

     b. How many words did you discover all told?

_____

     c. What is the commonest phonogram for /z/ among them?

_____

     d. How many times does it occur?

_____

e. Does this make a satisfactory parallel to your generalization for /f/, /l/, and /s/?

_____

f. Is it any more satisfactory if you consider only the most common of the words ending in /z/?

_____

2. Look up several words beginning with *x* in your dictionary, and then answer the following questions about them:

a. What seems to be their national origin?

_____

b. How is the *x* pronounced?

_____

c. The letter *x* appears at the beginning of a syllable other than an initial syllable only rarely. The only common example is *anxiety;* look it up in your dictionary and record here how the *x* is pronounced:

_____

3. English sometimes distinguishes between parts of speech in the same word by pronunciation. When the change is from /s/ to /z/ or vice versa, the sound of /z/ will always be represented by *s,* even when the /s/ is not, as in *advice* and *advise.* Below we have given you several examples of words with two pronunciations but one spelling. See how many more you can add:

close   house   abuse

_____

_____

_____

_____

_____

_____

Some people also distinguish in their speech between the two parts of speech of the following words:

grease   merchandise   rise

4. In column 1 we have given you examples of words ending in /z/ following one of the so-called long vowels. We have given examples of each of the vowel nuclei which are recognized by English spelling by being given special phonograms, and where possible we have given examples of both *s* and *z* words. A quick glance at the list will show you that there is no easy generalization to tell you which to use, but doing the following exercises will give you a few aids:

a. A careful examination of the list of words in column 1 will show that after certain sounds *z* never represents /z/; what are these sounds?

_____

b. One of the sounds you have just written down was also involved in a generalization in Chapter 12, exercise 4. What sound is it, and do you see any connection between this exercise and the earlier one?

_____

_____

c. The sound /aw/ may be represented, as we shall see later, by either *ou* or *ow*. We have given examples of both in our list in column 1 because the last word is almost the only one in which /z/ is represented by *z* following /aw/. Look up this word in your dictionary, or, if it is not there, one of its derivatives (*blowzed* or *blowzy*) and write out the definition here:

_____

_____

d. If you have a "Vocabulary of Rhymes" in your dictionary, look up the words which rhyme with those in column 1. In what length of word are you most likely to encounter *z* rather than *s?*

_____

e. The big exception to your preceding generalization is the large group of words ending in the suffix *-ize;* look it up in your dictionary, as it is a very useful combining form. Does your dictionary have a section dealing with the peculiarities of British spelling? If it does, what does it say about *-ise* and *-ize?*

_____

_____

5. From examining column 5, what would you say was the usual method of representing /z/ before /m/? Write out your conclusion below; it will be always correct at the end of the word, and almost always so when the two sounds appear elsewhere in the word:

_____

_____

6. The student should be reminded, even though the fact probably causes him no trouble in spelling, that the inflectional ending *-s* is often (though not always) pronounced /z/ as in *digs, toys, man's* (but cf. *cats*). Once again, being conscious of what you are dealing with when writing can help your spelling! Below write the sounds after which the inflectional *-s* sounds like /z/, giving an example each time:

_____

_____

Can you draw any conclusions as to what type of sound makes *-s* sound /s/, and what type of sound makes it /z/? (You might review here the pronunciation of *-ed,* and what makes it change its pronunciation.)

_____

16

/i/, /ɨ/, /ə/

It is time we turned our attention to some of the vowels again. As we said earlier, many people do not have both /i/ sounds in their speech, and even when they do, they cause little or no trouble in spelling. The speaker is conscious of using only one /i/ sound, and his only problems arise when he ceases to be aware that he is using an /i/ sound!

Occasionally situations arise in which the historical background is so interesting that we want to abandon the inductive method temporarily, and such an occasion arises with /ə/. One of the most troublesome aspects of this sound is the frequency with which it is represented by the letter *o* in the body of the word. There are several reasons for this, such as phonetic changes within the language itself, but the most interesting and the one providing one of the largest groups of examples, is what is sometimes known as "scribal *o*." During the Middle Ages the script employed, even when carefully written, easily confused *i, m, n, r,* and *u* (also used for *v* and *y*), so that many scribes adopted the practice of using an *o* for a *u* when any possibility of confusion arose, as in *son* (in Old English *sunu*). In dealing with scribal *o*, as with other problems connected with /ə/, the position of the sound in the word is important, as we shall see in the exercises.

Exercises

/i/ or /ɨ/

1	2	3	4	5	6
habit denim into	sleepy easy	bonnie stymie caddie corbie	pulley valley monkey money honey	spaghetti macaroni confetti broccoli	
	easily kindly				
			clayey		
	myth mystery		Charley		

1	2	3	4	5
under undo number	faculty republic cucumber	patriot demon havoc	hyena data drama	
	bimonthly handsomely uncover confronted	medium maximum minimum		
onion other oven		census focus		
		kingdom freedom		
		humorous ingenious credulous		

1. /i/ or /ɨ/ at the end of a word is troublesome for two reasons: English tends to avoid short vowels at the end of words, and so some users of the language slur over this final sound and make it resemble /ə/, as we have seen in the case of /æ/ also. Other users of the language fail to hear the final /i/ indicated in the pronunciation in their dictionary, but hear instead a sort of short-ened /iy/—actually /ɨ/. (This perhaps explains why so many students write *possible* for *possibly*.) In spite of this variation in pronunciation the following exercises should be helpful in straightening out the four possible spellings of /i/ or /ɨ/ at the end of a word:

 a. Look up the suffix -*ie* in your dictionary and write out here what it means:

 _____

 b. If your dictionary does not tell you in what dialect of English this suffix originated or at least is most prevalent, see how many words you can write down connected with the game of golf which end in -*ie* (there are two in the wordlists in column 3). Does this give you a hint as to where to expect the suffix?

 _____

 _____

 c. Look up in the dictionary the words in column 3 of the wordlists, and the words you wrote down in answering b.; are variant spellings given for them, and if so, what?

 _____

 _____

 d. What seems to be happening to these -*ie* endings? Does this suggest to you what the commonest phonogram for /i/ at the end of a word is?

e. Look up the suffix -*y* in your dictionary and write out here what it means:

_____

f. What do you do when you want to add this suffix to a word ending in *y,* such as *clay?*

_____

g. Look up the suffix -*ly* in your dictionary and write out here what it means:

_____

h. The suffixes -*ary,* -*ery,* and -*ory* are frequently confused because, being generally unaccented, they are pronounced much alike. Your dictionary will help you sort them out:

   (1) In what type of word are you most likely to find -*ary?*

_____

   (2) In what type of word will you find -*ery?*

_____

   (3) Differentiate, in your own words, between the commonest meanings of the suffixes as noun endings:

_____

_____

_____

i. Look up the suffix-*ey* in your dictionary and write out here what it means:

_____

j. What is happening to this suffix?

_____

k. Look at the first group of words in column 4 of the wordlists; there are fifteen or twenty more fairly common words like them which end in -*ey* when it is not a suffix. Where is the accent in these words?

_____

l. How do you form the plural of these words ending in -*ey* (or add an inflectional -*s* to verbs)?

_____

m. Look up the derivation of the words in column 5 of the wordlists; what does this tell you about *i* as a spelling for /i/ or /ɨ/ at the end of a word?

_____

74

n. In what type of word are you most likely to discover this spelling?

_____

2. a. Look up the derivations of the following words in your dictionary. What does your study suggest as to the national origin of words which use *y* instead of *i* for /i/ or /ɨ/ in the body of the word?

myth	crypt	oxygen	system	pyramid
rhythm	sibyl	analysis	polygon	pharynx

_____

b. In what two broad fields of learning are you most likely to encounter these words?

_____

3. /i/ or /ɨ/ is most troublesome when it appears in a final syllable followed by a single consonant sound. Words ending in /i/ followed by /b/, /d/, /g/, or /m/ are generally regular, as *glib, sprig, vivid,* and *maxim,* but when /i/ is followed by /l/, /n/, /s/, /t/, or /v/, you will need the help of these exercises:

a. Look up the suffix *-ive* in your dictionary. Remember the meaning, as it is a very useful and common suffix, but record here the pronunciation, and whether or not this is the pronunciation you would expect from this pattern of letters:

_____

b. The explanation of what you have just observed is the fact that no English word ever ends with the letter *v;* when the sound /v/ ends the word, the phonogram used is always *-ve.* (Why this is so is explained later in the chapter on English as a Phonetic Language, page 136). The *-ive* is not always a suffix, of course, and so occasionally the *i* represents a long sound, in which case there is no problem: for example, *hive.*

c. Look up the suffix *-ile* in your dictionary, and begin below a list of words which may be spelled *-il* (all words in which the end is not a suffix will be spelled this way):

_____

_____

_____

_____

d. Look up the suffix *-ine;* when may it be spelled *-in?*

_____

e. Continue the following lists of words ending in *-in* when the ending is not a suffix:

chagrin	moccasin	mandolin	violin

_____

_____

_____

f. The sounds /is/ as a suffix are always spelled -ice.

(1) How is the suffix -ise pronounced?

_____

(2) Can the e ever be dropped from the suffix -ice?

_____

g. When the ending is not a suffix, however, it may be spelled -ice, ise, or -is. You may find keeping a list of each group helpful (the majority of words in the third group will end in -sis; review Chapter 12, exercise 5d. here):

    pumice   promise   analysis

_____

_____

_____

h. Look up the suffix -ite in your dictionary. Many of its meanings are highly technical, and we may safely bypass them here. One common one is always pronounced with a long i and should be no problem. That leaves us with the words derived from past participles of Latin verbs, and unless you have had Latin in school, that information will not help much, because

(1) A number of English words ending in it are derived from the infinitive of Latin verbs, as permit (make a list of them here):

_____

_____

(2) Even among words ending in it derived from Latin past participles there are exceptions. Below are two; see if you can add to the list:

    benefit   explicit

_____

_____

(3) The suffix -ate, when unaccented, has been weakened until it sounds like /it/. Consequently the two suffixes are frequently confused, and the commonest misspelling of definite is *definate. You might make here a list of words which trouble you in this respect:

_____

_____

4. As though it had not provided enough trouble in its endings, /i/ provides more exotic representations of itself than any other short vowel. Here are a few to practice studying as demons—and remember that repeated reviews after lapses of time are especially effective.

sieve	build	women	busy	been
pretty	mountain	carriage	mischief	circuit

5. Knowledge of a few distinctions between pairs of prefixes and suffixes may help you out a little also:

    a. Write out here the difference in meaning between *dis-* and *dys-:*

_____

    b. Which of these prefixes are you more likely to encounter, and why?

_____

    c. What is the difference in meaning between the suffixes *-est* and *-ist?*

_____

    d. What is the distinction between *mis-* and *mys-?*

_____

6. We turn now to /ə/. At the beginning of a word, the spelling of this sound is fairly regular; in column 1 of the wordlists for /ə/ we have provided you with two groups of examples. The first is representative; the second is, so far as we know, complete.

    a. What, then, is your conclusion as to the usual method of representing /ə/ as the initial sound in a word?

_____

    b. Look up the three words in the second group; can you tell from their derivations which one has a scribal *o* in it?

_____

_____

7. In the middle of initial syllables (including the single syllables of one-syllable words) *u* is still the more common spelling. Many of the exceptions, however, may be remembered as groups:

    a. Prefixes with *o* followed by a consonant (i.e. not *pro-*) when they are unaccented tend to obscure the /a/ sound until it becomes very much like /ə/, as in *obscure, conform, comport.* Make a list here of such prefixes, with specimen words:

_____

_____

    b. Many of the other exceptions may be remembered by rhyming groups. We have begun a few for you below; continue them, and see if you can add other groups. Single words can also be jotted down here:

       brother   ton   one   honey   cover   some

_____

_____

_____

8. a. After inspecting the first group of words in column 2 of the wordlists, how do you think /ə/ is represented usually in the medial syllables of longer words (three or more syllables)?

_____

b. Are the words in the second group in the same column exceptions to the generalization you have just made, or to some other generalization?

_____

9. In a final syllable, /ə/ followed by a consonant is quite irregular, but knowledge of a few suffixes and word endings will straighten out most of the trouble:

a. Look up the suffix *-ous* and write out its meaning here; it is a very common suffix and provides almost the only examples of *ou* representing /ə/ in a final syllable:

_____

b. Look up the suffixes *-dom* and *-some* and write out their meanings below; a majority of the words having *o* for /ə/ in the final syllable have one of these suffixes:

_____

_____

c. The suffix *-ison* is not listed in many shorter dictionaries, but you will find it in unabridged ones. It is roughly equivalent to *-ation* in meaning, and appears in a few fairly common words such as *comparison, garrison, jettison,* and *venison.* The *o* is usually pronounced /ə/, so you may find it useful to extend this brief list below:

_____

_____

d. A large number of Latin words have come into English without changing their spelling; many of these end in either *-um* or *-us.* The latter are almost always nouns, while words ending in *-ous* are usually adjectives. This fact should be a help in choosing a spelling here. The ending *-um* almost never follows directly after a *d* or *s,* and so should not prove difficult to separate from the suffixes discussed in exercise b. This generalization is most true after *s;* the commonest exceptions follow *nd* as in *memorandum* and *referendum.* Record here any other exceptions to these statements which you can find:

_____

_____

10. English, as we have said, does not like to end words with a short vowel. The commonest spelling for /ə/ we have illustrated in column 4 of the wordlists.

a. Look up the plurals of the words ending in *-um* in column 3 of the wordlists; what you find will in part explain why *a* is the commonest phonogram for /ə/ at the end of a word.

b. What would you say was happening to these plurals?

_____

_____

11. /ə/ provides a number of demons in addition to the variations we have already listed; study the following individually:

touch	blood	does	double	tough
pigeon	porpoise	rough	flood	twopence

78

One of the most troublesome problems in spelling /ə/ is in choosing the right vowel letter for the suffixes *-ance* and *-ence, -ancy* and *-ency,* and *-ant* and *-ent.* As the same generalizations apply to all three pairs, we will illustrate with all three indiscriminately. We are providing wordlists and exercises for these suffixes.

1	2	3	4
significance	continuance	transference	residence
elegance	dominance	occurrence	accident
extravagance	exuberance	adherence	coincidence
applicant	ignorance	abhorrence	confidence
	radiance	coherence	evidence
	tolerance	deterrence	impudence
magnificence	conversant		
intelligence	recognizance		
innocence	ambulance		attendance
diligent	luxuriant		ascendant
indigence	variance		pendant
	suppliant		

5	6	7	8
expedience	excellence	omniscience	sufferance
lenience	benevolence	efficiency	petulance
experience	corpulence	sufficient	vigilant
convenient	equivalence	conscience	resistance
incipient	indolence		assistance
resilience	opulence		
sapience	prevalence	existence	
salient	insolence	subsistence	
	virulence	insistence	
		consistent	
		persistency	

1. Do the exercises following, which will help you in at least some of the commonest situations that arise when these letters are suffixes (which they aren't always).

   a. For column 1 of the wordlists review exercise 7 in Review Lesson V (page 150). Rewrite your generalization here:

   _____

   _____

   b. Column 2 should be mastered next, as many apparent exceptions to the other columns are explained by this column. All the words here have either (1) a companion word with an *a* in its suffix (*radiate, continuation, ignoramus*), or (2) a companion word ending in *-ize* or *-y* (*recognize, vary*). We'll tell you all this, as it would be too cumbersome to be inductive about this column.

c. In column 3, what sound precedes the suffix in the words, and where is the accent? Write your generalization here:

_____

Other words based on these same roots will also use -ence, etc., even though the accent has shifted as in *preference* and other words with *-fer.* A real exception is in column 8.

d. In column 4 what sound precedes the suffix in the words in the first group?

_____

e. In column 4 what two sounds precede the suffix in the words in the second group?

_____

_____

Write below your generalization about *both* groups:

_____

_____

These roots ending in *-nd* (you will find the half dozen commonest in our lists of Latin roots on pages 23 and 154) are quite erratic and irregular. Many allow both *-ant* and *-ent* spellings; look up all the meanings and spellings of *pendant,* for example.

f. In column 5 what sound precedes the suffix? Why is *alliance* not an exception to your generalization?

_____

_____

g. In column 6 what sound precedes the suffix? There are two common exceptions in column 8. Write your generalization here:

_____

_____

h. In column 7 the words in group 1 all have the same sound before the suffix (and *not* the same sound as in column 5); what is it?

_____

_____

Write your generalization here:

_____

_____

All of the second group in column 7 come from one Latin root, a fact which is somewhat unreliable as a spelling guide. The two commonest exceptions to the many words built on this root are in column 8.

2. The classical rule for spelling these suffixes is that roots derived from Latin verbs of the first and fourth conjugations (infinitives ending in *-are* and *-ire* respectively) used *-ance, -ancy,* and *-ant,* whereas roots derived from the second and third conjugations (infinitives ending in *-ēre* and *-ĕre*) used the other three. Go back now to the list of Latin roots on page 23, and write below two or three nouns ending in *-ance* or *-ence* for each root. Is the old classical rule a sound one?

_____

_____

_____

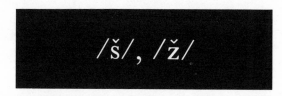

/š/, /ž/

The sound that we take up now is a single, distinctive sound in its own right, not a combination of /s/ and /h/, even though we use the symbol *sh* for it because of the limitations of our alphabet. When it is an original /š/ sound, it is usually represented by *sh*, and causes little trouble. But it is often the result of the palatalization of /s/ or /t/; when either of them precedes an /i/ sound followed by an unaccented or lightly accented /ə/, the tongue anticipates the palatal position of the /ə/ sound, and the *si* or *ci* or *ti* emerges as /š/.

The second sound is very much like our first, and frequently confused with it, yet keeping the two distinct may be very helpful to the speller. Disregarding the difference in accent and initial vowel sound, you will notice in the words *assure* and *azure* the difference in the sounds represented by the *ss* in *assure* and the *z* in *azure;* the former is the /š/ sound, the latter the /ž/ sound. Perhaps this almost-minimal pair will help to keep the two straight for you. The /ž/ sound is also frequently the result of palatalization, this time of /z/, but as /z/ is often represented by *s* (particularly between vowels) it may look as though /ž/ were a palatalization of /s/. Both sounds occur also in words of foreign origin—but let the wordlists and exercises try to simplify the spelling of these two sounds for you.

Exercises

/š/

1	2	3	4	5	6
finish	issue	machine	racial	martial	
tarnish	fissure	mustache	social	partial	
bishop		chute			
cashew		chivalry			
show	sure	brochure	ancient	tertian	
	insure		musician	Venetian	
	sumac				
			spacious	patient	
			gracious	quotient	
			ferocious		
			associate	facetious	
			enunciate	cautious	
				negotiate	
				minutia	

/ž/

1	2	3	4	5	6
azure seizure grazier	vision measure treasure usury	rouge garage barrage prestige	bijou		

1. Look up the etymologies of all the words in column 3 of the wordlists for /š/, and answer the following questions:

   a. What common national origin do these words have?

   _____

   b. What conclusion can you make as to when *ch* represents /š/?

   _____

   c. Can you think of any other words in which *ch* represents /š/?

   _____

   d. Look them up in the dictionary and see if they fit your generalization in question b. Do they?

   _____

2. Examples of /š/ caused by palatalization of /š/ may be found in columns 2, 4, and 5 of the wordlists. To help you with these we have prepared a few directive questions:

   a. In column 4 what immediately follows *ci* (which represents /š/ in these words)?

   _____

   b. In column 5 what immediately follows *ti* (which represents /š/ in these words)?

   _____

   c. Your problem, then, appears to be one of selecting the right phonogram in front of these endings. Go through the words in columns 4 and 5 and see how many of them have companion words (other parts of speech, etc.) which will give you a hint as to the spelling of /š/. How many could you find?

   _____

   d. The sound known as long *u* consists of an /i/ sound followed by a *w*-glide. This nucleus causes palatalization just as does any back vowel; some examples are given at the top of column 2. Can you add any more here?

   _____

   _____

e. The second group of words in column 2 is part of a small number of words in which the same phenomenon seems to occur even though the long *u* is accented. You should make a list of these; it will not be long:

_____

_____

f. The use of companion words as guides in spelling has its drawbacks, one of them being that you might think of the wrong word. For example, if you were asked to spell *differential,* you might think of either *different* or *difference,* and come up with a right or a wrong spelling, depending upon which word you used as a guide: all the many words ending in the suffix *-ance* or *-ence* and having a companion form in *-al* change the *ce* to *ti* before adding the *-al*— or, more properly speaking, add *-ial* to the adjective form in *-ant* or *-ent.*

g. Here are four candidates for the blank column 6: *spatial, palatial, financial, anxious.* From what you know already prepare to explain orally why each one of these is not the spelling you would expect (or, in one case, why the pronunciation of the word is not what you would expect).

3. As /ž/ is much less common a sound than /š/, we shall vary our method of questioning:

a. Look up the etymologies of all the words in column 3 of the wordlists for /ž/; what common national origin do these words all have?

_____

b. Can you make any generalization as to when *ge* represents /ž/, and in what part of the word?

_____

c. Can you think of any other examples?

_____

d. Look them up in the dictionary, and see if they fit your generalization in question b. Do they?

_____

e. The /ž/ sound in the word in column 4 is represented by *j*—a common spelling in French, where the sound is more usual than in English. Most appearances of it in our dictionary, such as *jeu d'esprit,* are still marked as foreign phrases. Can you add any English words to *bijou* in column 4?

_____

f. Both *s* and *z* can represent /ž/, as you can see in columns 1 and 2. We have made no attempt to sort out the examples of /ž/ which are the result of palatalization, but you can identify a few for yourself through companion words in which the *s* or *z* represents /z/. List any such pairs which you can find here:

_____

_____

_____

84

The only other place at which /ž/ and /š/ create a spelling problem is in the choice between the suffixes -sion and -tion. As this causes some students considerable trouble, we are providing special wordlists and exercises for it:

/šən/

1	2	3	4
beautification	passion	fraction	
education	discretion	election	
naturalization	expression	sanction	
completion	digression	junction	
devotion	abolition		
evolution	permission		
caution	submission	emulsion	
	discussion	propulsion	
	concussion		
		scansion	
	ashen	attention	
	freshen	extension	
		caption	
		deception	
		adoption	
		exemption	
		proscription	
		assumption	
		assertion	
		distortion	
		intorsion	

/žən/

1	2	3	4
evasion	division	aversion	
adhesion		diversion	
explosion		immersion	
confusion		submersion	

1. After inspecting the wordlists above, which are equally representative though unequal in length, how would you say /žən/ was always spelled?

_____

2. Can you make a similar generalization for /šən/?

_____

3. Compare the words in the two first columns above, in which the suffix always follows a long vowel. What spelling generalization can you make? Write it out below; it will be useful, because all the verbs ending in -ate, -fy, and -ize form nouns (if they form them at all) ending in /eyšən/:

_____

_____

4. The generalization when the suffix follows a short vowel is not so easy. For one thing, other suffixes intrude and create problems: -en added on to words already ending in sh, as in ashen and freshen; -ian added on to words ending in a quite different sound which then becomes /š/, as in musician and statistician. The following exercises should help you to select the right ending:

   a. After what two short vowels does -tion appear?

   _____

   b. How is -sion pronounced when it follows directly after a short vowel?

   _____

   c. When -sion is pronounced /šən/, what intervenes between it and the short vowel?

   _____

   d. *Passion,* the first word in the second column under /šən/, illustrates the dangers of using companion words; it has nothing to do with the verb *pass.* But a close inspection of these and other words ending in -ssion will show that many of them have companion verbs, close to them in meaning, which end in -ss, as express, discuss. For what short vowel does this last statement seem least applicable?

   _____

   e. Look back on page 76 and see if you can find a Latin root which will provide you with the explanation of why one short vowel seems to end its verbs in -t instead of -ss (the verbs are derived from the infinitive, the nouns from the past participle of the Latin verbs). Short /i/, of course, is the vowel with which you are concerned. Write out the Latin verb here, and an example of your own in English:

   _____

   f. Look up the suffixes -en and -ian; their meanings are so different from -tion or -sion that they should not confuse you if you keep your wits about you.

   _____

5. Following a consonant the suffix is very regular at times, and complicated at others:

   a. After what consonants will you always use -tion?

   _____

   b. After what consonants will you always use -sion?

   _____

   c. On page 23 you will find listed the three Latin roots which provide almost all of the examples of -tion after n (-sion is commoner). Write below as many words as you can think of ending in -tion and based on one of these three roots (better check with your dictionary too):

_____

_____

_____

_____

_____

d. In the fashion we have employed on page 23, write out below two or three Latin roots (infinitive and past participle), forms in which it appears in English, and examples of *-sion* following *n:*

_____

_____

e. For the suffix following *r,* inspect column 2 under /žən/. Do you pronounce the suffix as /žən/? If you do in all cases, this part of the spelling will cause you no trouble, for /žən/ is always spelled *-sion*. But for the many people who pronounce the suffix after *r* /šən/, there will be a problem. As *-sion* is the commoner spelling, perhaps the best plan is to make a list here of the words using *-tion:*

_____

_____

6. Below are six words ending in the sound /šən/ which might cause you some trouble. Study them as demons with your new method:

     coercion   complexion   fashion   ocean   stanchion   suspicion

7. Review exercise 6 in Chapter 5 for *-tion* after *s,* then explain why we have not discussed it in this chapter:

_____

_____

_____

_____

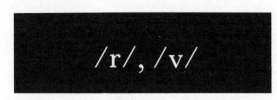

/r/, /v/

One of the most widespread dialectal variations in English is the omission of the sound of /r/—not universally, as many people think, but when followed by a consonant in the same or a closely following word. For example, the word *here* in "Here I am" is not pronounced in this speech as is the *here* in "Here they are." If this were all there were to it, there would be no spelling problem. But because so many words have two pronunciations for one spelling, the treatment has been extended to words having no /r/ originally, by adding the /r/ before the vowel. Thus *idea* rhymes with *here* as pronounced before a consonant; /r/ is added to *idea* before a vowel, and the two rhyme before a vowel also. This appearance and disappearance of /r/ can be confusing to a speller; if you use a dialect in which the omission and intrusion of /r/ is common, you must be on your guard. Even if you speak a dialect which sounds all the /r/'s, you may still have a little trouble with the sound, for it has a special phonogram of foreign origin which seems to cause difficulty for college students, and it has some dandy demons.

One of the most regular and least troublesome sounds is /v/ as in *very* and *over*. We have already encountered its greatest peculiarity (see page 75), namely, that the letter never ends a word. When the sound /v/ ends a word, as it often does, the phonogram used is *ve*. This is a holdover from the days when the letters *u* and *v* were interchangeable, and should be remembered when a consonant precedes the /v/, as in *carve* and *curve*; it creates problems, as we have already seen, when the vowel before the /v/ is short, as in the suffix *-ive*. Otherwise there are only one or two irregular words, one of them so short and common that you would probably forget about it, and so we have put it in the column of exceptions already.

Exercises

1	2	3	4	5	6
here there	error hurry	rhyme rhythm hemorrhage	vivid over oven gave	carve curve serve solve creative	of

1. Look up all the words in your dictionary beginning with the phonogram *rh,* and then answer the following questions:

    a. What does the national origin of most of these words seem to be?

    _____

    b. In what broad areas of learning are you most likely to encounter these words?

    _____

    c. Look up in your dictionary the combining forms beginning with *rrh* and write below as many words employing them as you know:

    _____

    _____

    rrh is the equivalent of *rr* in words of Greek origin, but only in words employing these combining forms will you ordinarily encounter it.

2. Most of us, I suspect, would include *separate* in a list of spelling demons, for that middle syllable /ər/ has caused quantities of trouble. Yet it is one of the commonest combinations of sounds in English, and, what is worse, has eight common spellings: *ar, er, ir, or, ur, yr, ear,* and *our.* As we try to unscramble these for you, you will doubtless be reminded of other demons as well as *separate.* We shall deal with /ər/ by position in the word here, and by phonogram in the Review Lesson.

    a. Look up in your dictionary a number of words *beginning* with each of the above eight phonograms. They are not always pronounced /ər/, of course; in an accented syllable it will probably be marked *ûr,* and *ēr* or *ər* in an unaccented syllable. Pronunciation varies from dialect to dialect too, from /er/ to /ər/; we shall simplify by using /ər/ as our symbol. Which of the eight phonograms represent /ər/ initially in a word?

    _____

    b. When /ər/ occurs in an initial syllable preceded by a consonant, your knowledge of prefixes will help considerably:

        (1) Look up *ser-* and *sur-* in your dictionary, and count the number of words beginning with each; which one are you more likely to meet and why?

        _____

        (2) Look up *per-* and *pur-* in your dictionary, and count the number of words beginning with each; which one are you more likely to encounter and why?

        _____

        (3) The sounds /sər/ may also be represented by *cir-.* This is not a prefix, but look at the words in your dictionary beginning with this combination of letters to see under what limited circumstances it will appear. What are they?

        _____

        (4) A prefix which usually has the /ər/ sound in the *second* syllable is *inter-;* what is the difference in meaning between it and *intra-?*

        _____

c. Because of the commonness of certain suffixes, the /ər/ combination probably appears most frequently at the end of words:

(1) What, if anything, does your dictionary tell you about *-ar, -er,* and *-or* as noun suffixes and their differences in meaning?

_____

(2) What other very common meaning is there for the suffix *-er?*

_____

(3) What is the difference between the suffixes *-ward* and *-wards?*

_____

(4) Some words end in *-ar, -er, -or,* and *-ard* when these endings are *not* suffixes. We have begun lists of such words for you here; see how many you can add:

vinegar	infer	metaphor	hazard

_____

_____

_____

(5) Other words that end in /ər/ have spellings which are never suffixes, such as *-ir* and *-ur.* See how many words you can add to these lists which we have begun for you:

whir			occur

_____

_____

d. In medial syllables the common spelling for /ər/ is *er,* a fact which probably explains why *separate* and other words which do *not* use *er* are difficult to remember. Word analysis will help in many cases; for example, what do the following words have in common in their structure?

discourage	rehearsal	confirmation

_____

3. Make a list here of words which end with a short vowel followed by *-ve,* excluding words ending in the suffix *-ive,* which provides most of the examples. Some of the others are so common you will probably miss them; so we have started rhyming groups for you:

have	give	above

_____

_____

/e/, /u/

/e/ and /u/ are much simpler than the last vowels we took up. Aside from the usual crop of demons, there is only one sizable group for each vowel that may cause some trouble. About forty common words descended from Old English have not kept step in their spelling with phonetic changes in their vowel sounds, and represent /e/ by *ea* as a result. Ten or a dozen rhyme with *head,* and other smaller rhyming groups can be formed, but most of these words you probably know already. With /u/ the trouble is likely to arise from the words using *u* to represent the sound.

Exercises

1	2	3	4	5	6
end	feather	book	full	gourmet	heifer
pet	weather	foot	hopeful	tourist	leopard
well	breadth	stood	bullet	could	friend
whether		wool	put	your	any
			bush		said
					wolf
					woman

1. A good half of all the words employing *ou* to represent /u/ begin with either *gour-* or *tour-;* look up in your dictionary all the words beginning with these two sets of phonograms, and then do the following exercises:

   a. What is the national origin of these words in which *ou* is pronounced /u/?

   b. Look up the pronunciation and derivation of *could, should, would,* and *your.* (The pronunciation of *your* varies from /yer/ to /yǝr/ to /yuwr/, depending upon the amount of stress placed upon it, and the dialect of the speaker; we include it here because the dictionaries apparently find /yur/ a common middle ground and list it as the pronunciation.) Do they fit your generalization in question a.?

c. Can you think of any other words in which *ou* represents /u/? Do they support your generalization in a.? Write them, and their national origin, below:

2. In the column of exceptions (6) we have listed two of the very few words which, with their compounds and derivatives, have *o* to represent /u/. Can you add any to this list?

3. There is no good generalization to help you choose between *oo* and *u* for /u/, but the following exercises may provide you with some helpful pointers:

   a. Look up the meanings of the suffix *-hood*, and write out here some illustrations of its usage not given by your dictionary in the entry under *-hood:*

   b. Look up the meanings of the suffix *-ful* (you might review Chapter 10 also, to discover why the suffix has only one *l*), and write out here some illustrations of its usage not given by your dictionary in the entry under *-ful:*

   c. Except for *wolf, wool,* and their compounds and derivatives, /u/ is always represented by *u* before /l/. Are *could, should,* and *would* exceptions to the preceding statement? Explain:

4. Write below each of the following words as many words as you can think of which are eye-rhymes as well as ear-rhymes of the words given:

   feather   pleasure   health   death

5. If you have not already mastered them anyway, these demons will require a little individual attention:

   heifer   leopard   friend   any   said   says

92

/h/, /w/, /hw/

The letter *h* is troublesome to spellers on two accounts; it forms a part of several digraphs or trigraphs where it has no independent value (as in *ch, gh, ph, tch,* and so on); and the sound of /h/ has a habit of disappearing, not only in Cockney but in practically all dialects of English as well. To counterbalance this, the sound always appears at the beginning of a syllable, which fact sometimes helps in syllabication.

Words which came into English from Old French, where the /h/ had already been lost, never had the sound, of course. A few of them, like *able* and *abundant,* had even lost the *h* in spelling too by the eighteenth century. Then during the eighteenth century an attempt was made to restore the /h/; it succeeded with some less common words; with others usage today wavers, as in *herb, homage,* and *hotel.* And even though the commonest, such as *honest, honor,* and *hour,* still lack the /h/, the eighteenth-century tampering with the language has left a state of considerable confusion for the speller.

Furthermore, most words, whether from Old French or not, tend to weaken or drop entirely the /h/ at the beginning of unaccented syllables. For example, compare the pronunciations of *prohibit* and *prohibition.* Comparisons of this sort may often provide you with a clue as to whether or not there is an *h* in a word. This same tendency is extended to include /h/'s which may be accented in the word itself, but not in the sentence in which it is used. The pronouns and auxiliary verbs beginning with *h* (*he, him, his, her, has, had, have,* etc.) are the most obvious examples. It is sometimes useful to try using a troublesome word in different sentences to see what a change of emphasis will do to the /h/. For example, compare the pronunciations of *historical* in these two sentences: "Historical research is important," and "This is an historical document of importance." You are much more likely to hear the /h/ in the first sentence.

The letter *w* is one of two in English which may represent either a consonant or a vowel. We have already discussed /w/ as a glide at the end of some vowel nuclei, and shall do so again. Now we shall consider it only as a consonant, when it occurs only at the beginning of syllables, and only before vowels, never before consonants. The letter is reasonably regular, and causes little difficulty except to students who cannot hear the difference between /w/ and /hw/ or when it becomes silent.

The representation of /hw/ by *wh* is the only example of many Old English reversals which has established itself as standard English on a wide scale. (Other examples are in exercise 4 in Review Lesson 1.) In Old English, for example, *what* was spelled *hwaet.* But by approximately 1225 an English monk named Orm, the earliest spelling reformer writing in English, was spelling the sounds *wh* consistently, and gradually (not necessarily because of his influence) this spelling has become general. If you look through the derivations of words beginning with *wh* you will find many illustrations of this change, and you will also see that English-speaking people have long had trouble distinguishing between /hw/ and /w/; in many dialects of English today are words in which /w/ has been substituted for /hw/.

Exercises

1	2	3	4	5	6
haste hate	hour honor honest	watch well		what when where why	sword
			write wreck wren		
		swing sway twinge whine			
prohibit comprehend	prohibition philharmonic shepherd		two who whoop		
		dowager charwoman			
			answer boatswain coxwain towards		

1. Look up in your dictionary or in a guide to English usage the distinction between the indefinite articles *a* and *an;* write out below when you should use each one:

_____

2. Put a circle around each silent *h* in the following words, and be prepared to explain orally why each one is silent:

ghost	shepherd	humor	forehead	hotel
honor	vehement	gherkin	horror	honest

3. You should be able to identify one of the times *w* is silent by inspecting the following ten words. Write out your generalization below them:

write	wreck	wrestle	wrong	wreak
wrapper	wriggle	written	wren	wrangle

_____

_____

4. The *w* is silent under other circumstances also. Compare the second group of words in column 3 with the second group in column 4 and the single word in column 6. Can you figure out when the *w* is silent? Write your generalization below:

_____

_____

This generalization actually involves only words beginning with /h/, /s/, and /t/. It is unsatisfactory only for words beginning with /s/; can you list some exceptions here?

_____

_____

5. The *w* is silent also in group 3 of column 3; by comparing the following pairs of words can you tell when it is silent? Write your generalization below, and any other examples of this type of silent *w* that you can discover:

answer	boatswain	coxwain
forswear	swain	swain

_____

_____

6. The tendency to drop the /h/ in words beginning with /hw/ is growing. If the /h/ is omitted from the following words, the resulting word has a homonym which means something else. Write the homonym below each word, and test yourself on your pronunciation, so that you will know how much to be on guard in choosing the right word and spelling:

when	whether	where	whine

_____

whet	whit	whoa	whir

_____

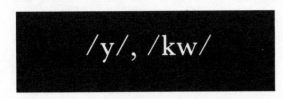

/y/, /kw/

We begin this lesson with the second of the two sounds in English which can be either vowel or consonant. Like /w/, /y/ forms the glide at the end of many vowel nuclei; before a vowel it is called a consonant. And like /w/, consonantal /y/ can appear only before vowels. It is commonly spelled *y* as in *year* and *beyond,* or *i* as in *onion* and *poniard.* Although *y* is the Anglo-Saxon spelling, *i* is today just as common. We shall have occasion to mention consonantal /y/ again when we come to what is usually known as long *u,* in which the first element is either short or barred /i/, each of which may be easily confused with consonantal /y/. Until then, just remember that there is not a *y* every time you seem to hear one—for example, *use, unite,* and *value.*

The consonant combination /kw/ was regularly represented by *cw* in Old English, but under the influence of the French introduced into England by the Norman invasion, the French digraph *qu* took over, not only in words of French origin but in native words as well. For example, the word that was spelled in Old English *cwic* is now spelled *quick.* We include this combination more for the sake of completeness than because it causes difficulty, for /kw/ is usually represented by *qu.* Just remember, however, that *qu* sometimes represents a sound or combination of sounds other than /kw/.

Exercises

1	2	3	4	5
yes	onion	vignette	quick	choir
yet	poniard	mignonette	quiet	awkward
year	union	chignon	queen	bookworm
yeast			request	
yard			quire	
yield			require	
yoke				
youth				
beyond				

1. a. Look up the pronunciation of *vignette* and *mignonette,* two relatively recent borrowings from French. How is the consonantal /y/ represented in these words?

b. Look up the pronunciation and derivation of *onion* and *poniard,* two older borrowings from French. How is the consonantal /y/ represented in these words?

_____

c. Make a list (it won't be long) either here or in column 3 above of all the words you can think of or encounter which use *gn* to represent /n/ followed by consonantal /y/:

_____

_____

2. In some dialects of English the consonantal /y/ intrudes itself as a glide between a consonant and the following vowel where in other dialects it does not appear. These two exercises may help you be on your guard in spelling:

a. Look up the pronunciation of the following words, in which consonantal /y/ is frequently heard; underline those in which your dictionary uses the /y/, circle those in which *you* use it:

    alien   column   linear   champion   coupon

b. A very common place for the intrusion of /y/ is after /d/ and before /ə/, with the resulting palatalization of /d/ into /j/. (You might review exercise 5 in Chapter 6 here.) Look up the pronunciation of the following words, underlining those in which the dictionary uses a /y/ and circling those in which *you* use the /y/ *or* palatalize the /d/:

    invidious   tremendous   commodious   hazardous   pendulum

    studious   hideous   tedious   stupendous   schedule

After you finish this exercise, look back at your answer to exercise 6 in Chapter 6.

3. In an earlier lesson (Chapter 11, exercises 4 and 10) you learned that *qu* (and *que*) could represent another sound than /kw/ or /kwe/.

a. What is this sound?

_____

b. Give some examples of words in which *qu* represents this sound:

_____

c. Give some examples of words in which *que* represents this sound:

_____

4. The only common exceptions to the statement that /kw/ is always represented by *qu* are the words which stand at the head of column 5 in our wordlists. One has a perfectly regular homonym, *quire;* look up the meanings of both these words so that you will use the right one at the right time. Then study *choir* as you would any other demon. Look up the derivation of *awkward,* and you will perhaps understand how *kw* occasionally comes to represent /kw/ in such words as this one and *bookworm.*

/ŋ/, /ð/, /θ/

In this and the next lesson we take a final look at some consonants: today at three individual consonant sounds which, though common enough, rarely cause any trouble in spelling; next time at some consonant combinations which are occasionally misleading, though fortunately not too common.

The first of these single consonant sounds is one which many people think of as a combination or blend of two consonants because it is most frequently represented by a digraph, *ng*, which in the International Phonetic Alphabet is represented by an *n* with a tail on it /ŋ/. There is, generally, little trouble when the *g* is present in the spelling, but before /g/, /k/, or /z/ the sound may be represented by *n* alone. Not every *n* before /g/, /k/, or /z/ will be pronounced /ŋ/, but whenever you do hear /ŋ/ before one of these sounds, you may be sure it will be spelled *n*.

As we have already seen (pages 7–8), the phonogram *th* actually represents two different sounds: compare them in *thin* and *this*, or *breath* and *breathe*. Old English had two symbols for these sounds, but (as you may see in more detail if you care to read Chapter 33) under French influence *th* took over for both. Today little distinction is made between the sounds in spelling. When *t* and *h* appear together but in separate syllables, each has its own sound, of course, as in *nut·hatch* and *court·house*.

Exercises

1	2	3	4	5
sing	bank	thin	this	
sang	uncle	breath	breathe	
sung	anchor	cloth	clothe	
song	anxious	cloths	clothes	
strong	distinct	mouth (n.)	mouth (vb.)	
length	conquer			
	anxiety			
	anger			
	angle			
	finger			
	jingle			
	longer			
	hunger			
	jungle			

1. This exercise, contrary to our usual custom, is concerned with non-rhyming words. According to the dictionary, the following pairs of words do not rhyme. Put a circle around the word in which the *n* represents /ŋ/:

finger   longer   anger

singer   wronger   hangar

2. When *ng* is followed by a silent *e* what happens? Look at the following words and see if you can write in below them the generalization covering them (if not, review Chapter 6):

change   revenge   singe   lunge   lounge

_____

_____

3. In columns 3 and 4 of the wordlists we have given you some illustrations of the fact that a few words shift from one *th* sound to the other to indicate a change in part of speech (noun and verb, for example). This creates the only real problem with *th*, because *sometimes,* but not always, one will have a silent *e* added. Below are the commonest words with the silent *e* in one form; write the form not given beneath it, and indicate the part of speech of each:

bathe   wreath   teeth   sheathe   loath   soothe

_____

After completing this exercise you might review exercises 5, 6, and 7 in Chapter 1.

/gz/, /gž/, /kš/

The three combinations of sounds shown above we are taking up together because they are most commonly represented by *x*. Except for /kš/, in fact, they have no other form of representation. When /k/ appears before the suffix *-tion*, a /kš/ combination is produced as in *connection* and *complexion*. But as we have already dealt with these words, and /kš/ in this situation, in Chapter 17, we shall disregard them now. You may assume that all remarks about /kš/ in today's lesson apply to it when *-tion* is not involved.

The letter *x*, when it follows an accented vowel, is normally pronounced /ks/, as we have seen. When it follows an unaccented vowel it is often pronounced /gz/ rather than /ks/, as in *exact* and *exist*, the extent to which /gz/ is used varying from one dialect to another and one speaker to another. But if a /ə/ or /u/ follows the *x*, the sound it represents may become palatalized: /ks/ will become /kš/ as in *anxious* and *luxury*; /gz/ will become /gž/ as in *luxurious*. In most dialects, however, these will not occur often enough to bother your spelling. Keep a list of these palatalizations in the wordlists and you will be well protected. Occasionally pairs of words like *luxury* and *luxurious* influence one another's pronunciation: *luxury* is heard with a /gž/ combination, or *luxurious* is heard with /kš/. As the spelling is *x* in either word, however, this should not trouble you.

Exercises

1	2	3	4
exact exempt exhaust exist exorbitant exult	luxurious	luxury anxious	

1. Look up the pronunciations given in your dictionary for all the words beginning with *ax-*, *ix-*, *ox-*, and *ux-*, and then answer the following questions:

   a. When are you most likely to run into /gz/?

   _____

   b. How sound is the generalization you have just made?

   _____

2. Look up the pronunciations of all the words beginning with *exi-* or *exu-*. Then answer the following questions:

    a. How many of these words have either /gž/ or /kš/ given as the preferred pronunciation for *x?*

_____

    b. How frequently do you think you will encounter these combinations?

_____

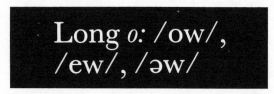

24

Long *o:* /ow/, /ew/, /əw/

With this lesson we take leave of the simple vowels and consonants, and begin work on the vowel nuclei, or long vowels as we shall continue to call them, using the old expression as a generic term for the nuclei represented by the same group of phonograms. We remind you of what we said back on pages 11–12 about the pattern of phonograms for each long vowel. The letter which "says its own name" (as the primers used to explain) is used alone at the end of syllables other than final syllables. At the end of final syllables one special phonogram, and often two phonograms, have been developed. And two different phonograms appear regularly in syllables ending in a consonant, with a preference for one of these for use in the body of the word and the other in the final syllable, although the strength of this preference varies considerably from one vowel to another. No long vowel fits this ideal plan perfectly, but as long *o* comes as near to it as any, we shall begin with it.

Long *o* is most commonly created in America with the /o/ of *gonna* followed by the *w*-glide. The very "British" British speech uses an /e/ followed by the *w*-glide. A few eastern American dialects, the best known of which is one heard frequently in and around Philadelphia, employ /ə/ before a *w*-glide.

At the famous Abbey Theatre in Dublin, the student actors and actresses cannot appear on the stage in a professional production until they can speak three Irish dialects fluently. For a moment pretend you are a student actor, and practice pronouncing *go, no,* and *so* with these three different nuclei. If you have a friend from Philadelphia available, it will help to have him pronounce these words for you if you use another nucleus normally.

Exercises

1	2	3	4	5	6
motion	home	boat	toe	tow	door
donate	prose	coast	foe	glow	old
odor	denote	road	woe	blow	roll
October	vote	roar	throe	throw	soul
locomotive	promote	loaf	roe	row	course
	console	loam	sloe	slow	gross
	postpone	hoarse	hoe	grow	though
					plateau

(continued)

1	2	3	4	5	6
go	boredom	coarsen	roebuck	arrow	
no	forecast	coating	woeful	shallow	
so	wholesome	roadster	mistletoe	tomorrow	
piano	stokehold	soapstone	tiptoe	bungalow	
potato	boneless	overload			
tomato					
Negro			oboe	slowly	
folio				crowbar	
gigolo				towhead	
embryo				known	
studio				growth	
banjo					
buffalo				bowl	

1. From inspecting the first five columns in our wordlists, can you tell which column contains:

   a. the words in which *o* represents long *o*?

   _____

   b. the phonogram which represents long *o* at the end of multi-syllabic words?

   _____

   c. the phonogram which represents long *o* followed by a consonant primarily in one-syllable words?

   _____

   d. the phonogram which represents long *o* followed by a consonant at the end of multi-syllabic words also?

   _____

   e. the phonogram which is the "extra" in the ideal pattern of phonograms?

   _____

   What does this phonogram do?

   _____

2. Looking at the above sections of columns 2 and 3, and assuming (as you may) that these are typical words, what is your conclusion about long *o* followed by a consonant in syllables other than the final syllable? Write your conclusion here:

   _____

   _____

3. Similarly, look at columns 4 and 5:

   a. When do *-oe* and *-ow* end syllables other than final syllables?

   _____

b. There is one exceptional word in each of these columns; identify each and explain why it is exceptional:

(1) _____

(2) _____

4. The list of words ending in *o* in column 1 contains all the common examples; can you add any to the list?

_____

_____

5. Certain sounds, mainly /l/, /r/, and /w/, influence the sounds immediately before or after them. We have already seen /w/ at work on /or/, turning it into /ər/ in such words as *world* and *worth*. Normally, when two consonants follow a single vowel letter, that vowel is short. But after the letter *o*, either the letter *l* or *r* plus a second consonant leaves the vowel long. These words can best be learned by rhyming families; we have started you on four below, and you can begin others as you need them. In some situations *o* will always be the spelling for long *o*; in others there may be two or more possibilities (for example, *horse* and *hoarse*; *coarse* and *course*). Just remember that before /l/ or /r/ plus a second consonant, long *o* may be represented by *o*. Here are four quite regular rhyming families to practice on; see how many words rhyming with these four you can write below them:

old   colt   form   torn

_____

_____

_____

_____

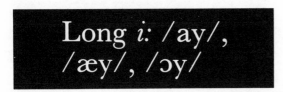

25

Long *i:* /ay/, /æy/, /ɔy/

The sound of long *i* is commonly created in two ways in America. In northern and western dialects an /a/ followed by the *y*-glide makes this sound as in *time* and *tide;* in southern dialects an /æ/ followed by the *y*-glide produces the sound used in their pronunciation of these words. /ɔ/ followed by a *y*-glide, although phonetically closer to the sounds represented by *oi* than to long *i,* is used in the dialects in which it appears for long *i.* For speakers of these dialects (mostly Irish) this fact may cause some trouble unless they are careful.

So far as the spelling is concerned, long *i* presents a somewhat different pattern from long *o,* but not much more difficult to master in its general outlines.

Exercises

1	2	3	4	5	6
spider	fine	nigh	by	hyphen	tie
tiny	smile	high	try	cycle	bye
final	twice	sigh	spry	dynamo	buy
library	concise	thigh	why	hydrogen	bind
denial	incline		wry		lisle
society					
		light		type	
	hireling	plight	deny	style	
alibi	likeness	fright	rely	pyre	
alkali	fireproof		imply		
	spikenard		gratify		
		delight		analyze	
		insight		paralyze	
		limelight		neophyte	
		foresight		enzyme	
		lightning		stereotype	

1. After studying the wordlists, particularly the first five columns, answer these questions:
   a. What phonogram is used for long *i* most frequently at the end of syllables other than final syllables?

   _____

   b. What other phonogram is also used in this place?

   _____

c. Can you think of any other examples than the two given of words which end in long *i* spelled *i*?

_____

d. What is the usual spelling for long *i* at the end of words?

_____

e. What is the usual spelling for long *i* in a syllable ending in a consonant?

_____

f. What digraphs or trigraphs are used for long *i*?

_____

g. What is the national origin of the words in column 5?

_____

h. In what ways is the use of the phonogram in column 3 limited? (You might be interested in looking up the etymology of *delight* in an unabridged dictionary, and finding out where the *gh* came from, before you answer this question.)

_____

i. Is the phonogram in column 2 limited in the same way?

_____

j. Under what circumstances do you find long *i* in a syllable ending in a consonant other than in a final syllable?

_____

k. Into what rhyming families do the words in column 3 seem to fall?

_____

2. There are a lot of one-syllable words which end in long *i*, and you have a choice of five possible phonograms from which to select the right one. A combination of one generalization and five rhyming families may help you, however. Below these five words write as many eye- and ear-rhymes as you can think of for each, and then answer the questions farther down:

| try | pie | nigh | bye | buy |

_____

_____

_____

_____

_____

_____

a. What phonogram is always used after two or more consonant *sounds* (remember that a digraph such as *th* in *thigh* may represent only one consonant sound)?

_____

b. In what words is this same phonogram used following only one consonant sound?

_____

c. What phonogram is the next most common of the five?

_____

d. Which group has only four common words? Learn them:

_____

e. Which group has only three common words? Learn them:

_____

f. Which group has only two common words? Learn them:

_____

(And always, when dealing with homonyms as you will be here, learn the meanings with the spellings.)

3. Two other groups of rather exceptional words may best be dealt with through rhyming families; see how many eye- and ear-rhymes you can find to go with these words:

hind   lisle

_____

_____

26

Long *e:* /iy/, /ɨy/

The sound known as long *e* is remarkably consistently spoken almost everywhere. In most places it is a short *i* followed by a *y*-glide. In a few dialects, the best known once again being from the Philadelphia area, the sound is barred /i/ followed by the *y*-glide. If you do not speak this dialect yourself, you may find it interesting to ask a fellow-student from around Philadelphia to pronounce for you *be, me,* and *see,* and notice carefully how his long *e* differs from yours.

Pronunciation will probably not cause the speller much trouble, but the abundance of phonograms to choose from may. We have had to divide our wordlists into two sections this time; below are those for the four commonest phonograms, while on the next page are those for three others and the column of exceptions.

Exercises

1	2	3	4
secret	these	heat	meet
veto	theme	weak	steel
prefix	scene	leave	queen
being	accede	clean	teeth
equal	supersede	ease	sleep
panacea	serene		
		appeal	exceed
be		reveal	proceed
simile		increase	succeed
recipe		release	canteen
aborigine			
catastrophe		easy	sleepy
		eastern	sheepskin
		heater	beetle
		peacemaker	steeple
		eagle	fleecy
		deacon	
			bee
		flea	flee
		lea	lee
		sea	see
		bohea	agree
			referee
			pedigree

5	6	7	8
ceiling	chief	oblique	people
conceit	grief	critique	
deceit	grieve	automobile	
receipt	siege	ravine	
conceive	shriek	routine	
deceive	field	marine	
perceive	lien	gasoline	
receive	fiend	magazine	
seize	bier	sardine	
seizure	tier	caprice	
leisure	cashier	police	
either	financier	cerise	
neither	cavalier	valise	
weir	niece	elite	
weird	priest	fatigue	
sheik	frieze	regime	
		naive	

1. After studying the wordlists, particularly the first four columns, answer these questions:

   a. What phonogram is used for long *e* most frequently at the end of syllables other than final syllables?

   _____

   b. What other phonograms are also used in this place?

   _____

   c. What seems to be the commonest phonogram for long *e* at the end of a word?

   _____

   d. What other phonograms are used here also?

   _____

   e. How many other examples of these last can you add to those already given in the word-lists?

   _____

   f. Can you make a generalization as to which phonogram to use to represent long *e* when it is followed by a consonant in a final syllable?

   _____

   _____

   g. From looking at the very representative group of words in column 2, where would you expect to find the *e*-consonant-silent-*e* pattern representing long *e* in a word?

   _____

109

h. What phonograms most frequently represent long *e* followed by a consonant in syllables other than final ones?

i. Where in a word can the phonograms *ea* and *ee* be used?

j. What is the meaning of the suffix *-ee,* and how frequently do you think you will be encountering it?

k. The three phonograms illustrated in columns 5, 6, and 7 are used much less frequently than those we have been discussing, and consequently our wordlists are much more thorough. After what letter does the phonogram in column 5 appear a majority of the time?

l. The phonogram in column 6 is used only before certain sounds; we have illustrated each one. What are they?

This information is not much positive help, but the process of elimination can be of real assistance to a speller at times.

m. The phonogram in column 7 is used only before certain sounds also; we have illustrated each one once, the commonest ones more frequently in proportion to their frequency. List the sounds below, starring the commonest:

n. Where does the phonogram in column 7 always appear?

o. What is the national origin of this phonogram?

p. What is the difference in meaning between the suffixes *-ier* and *-eer?*

2. In column 4 are the three verbs which end in *-ceed;* in column 2 is the one word which ends in *-sede.* All the other words which end in the same sounds are spelled *-cede.* Below write the one *-sede* word, the three *-ceed* words, and as many *-cede* words as you can think of:

3. The list in column 5 is a fairly complete list of the commonest words in which *ei* represents long *e.* Many of these fit into rhyming groups and can be most easily remembered that way. See how many words you can add to the lists we have begun for you:

deceit	receive	leisure	either

_____

_____

_____

_____

_____

And except for derivatives such as *breather* in the last group, all words in these patterns follow these spellings.

4. Although more words use *ie* than *ei* for long *e,* the rhyming groups can still be useful. Try to add as many eye-rhymes as well as ear-rhymes to the following lists as you can:

yield	thief	believe

_____

_____

_____

Many of the verbs in the third column will have companion nouns in the second. Except for the first column, these lists do not represent all the spellings of ear-rhyming words (*leaf* and *leave,* for example), and with the first column we have to assume that past participles "don't count," as *revealed* and *peeled.* These groups are, nonetheless, convenient ways for remembering the many fewer words which use *ie.*

5. List below all the one-syllable words you can think of which end in *e*-consonant-silent-*e.* What is your conclusion as to the usual place for this pattern to appear?

_____

_____

_____

_____

6. As the pronunciation of sounds and even of entire words varies from dialect to dialect and person to person, it is at times hard to know where to include certain phonograms or words. If you are one of the people who hears a long *e* at the end of words ending in unaccented *-ie* or *-ey,* you should review what we said about them in the lesson on short *i,* and make a list here of those you encounter frequently:

_____

_____

_____

7. Defying all generalizations and falling into no nice rhyming groups, these demons are fine words for you to practice your special method of study on:

people   debris   alumnae   quay   key

_____

_____

_____

_____

_____

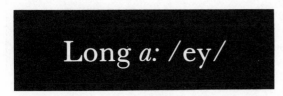

27

Long *a:* /ey/

The sound of long *a,* the sound of the name of the letter, is quite generally made with /e/ followed by a *y*-glide, as in *day* and *play*. The pronunciation of this sound is not likely to cause any trouble, but the written representation of the sound is so varied that once again we have to divide our wordlists into two parts. Fortunately some of the phonograms are quite limited in their use, and others are much more regular in their behavior than were those for long *e,* so our generalizations should be of more help.

Exercises

1	2	3	4
gravy	brake	mail	gray
baker	grate	slain	stray
datum	stake	quaint	play
haven	wave	raid	day
bacon	safe	waif	gay
able	rage	claim	spray
hiatus	gale	bait	relay
vacation			decay
			essay
	mistake	dainty	portray
	ingrate	daisy	roundelay
	palisade	fairy	
	balustrade	raisin	
		maiden	crayon
		plaintiff	payment
	blameless	wainscot	layman
	bracelet		wayward
	trademark		essayist
		acclaim	
		bewail	
		sustain	
		domain	

5	6	7	8
break	feint	they	straighten
great	geisha	bey	
steak	heir	fey	
yea	inveigle	grey	
bear	obeissance	prey	
pear	surveillance	trey	
tear	their	whey	
wear	veil	obey	
	vein	disobey	
	skein	convey	
breaker	seine	purvey	
breakfast	rein	survey	
breakneck		strathspey	
greatly			
greatness	deign		
beefsteak	feign		
bearbaiting	reign		
	weigh		
	weight		
	eight		
	eighteen		
	neigh		
	neighbor		
	inveigh		
	freight		
	sleigh		

1. In order to review the general remarks which we made in Chapter 1 and at the beginning of these lessons on the long vowels inspect the wordlists carefully, and then answer briefly these questions about long *a*:

a. What phonogram most commonly represents long *a* at the end of a word? (The first four columns are representative only; the last three are relatively complete for their phonograms.)

_____

b. What phonogram most commonly represents long *a* at the end of syllables other than final ones?

_____

c. What phonogram most commonly represents long *a* in syllables ending in a consonant, primarily in monosyllables and the final syllables of longer words?

_____

d. What phonogram represents long *a* most commonly in syllables ending in a consonant, primarily in monosyllables and the early syllables of longer words?

_____

e. Under what circumstances will the phonogram discussed in question c. appear in other than final syllables?

_____

f. Under what circumstances is the phonogram mentioned in question d. most likely to appear in the final syllable of a multisyllabic word?

_____

g. This same phonogram occasionally ends a syllable other than a final syllable. You studied three examples in exercise 11, Chapter 2; write them and any others you can think of below. What do these three suggest as to the circumstances under which this phonogram will end a syllable other than a final syllable?

_____

2. Fundamentally, only eight words use _ea_ to represent long _a;_ all the others are compounds or derivatives of these eight. All but _yea_ have homonyms or homographs, these latter being words of different derivation and meaning and sometimes, as here, different pronunciation, but the same spelling. Below each of the following words write a homonym or a homograph, being sure you know the meaning of each word in the pair:

     break   great   steak   bear   pear   tear   wear

_____

3. The phonogram _ei_ is only slightly more common than _ea_ when they are sounded as long _a._ Our list is fairly complete for the more common words, which can best be learned through rhyming families and through pairs and trios of homonyms. We have also included in the same list the words with _eigh_ as a phonogram for long _a;_ you will remember that _igh_ was a phonogram for long _i._ Can you answer these questions?

a. Do the words with _eigh_ for long _a_ have the same limitations as the words with _igh_ for long _i?_

_____

b. In _deign, feign,_ and _reign,_ is the _g_ part of the phonogram which represents long _a_ or not?

_____

4. a. Where does the accent fall in the words in column 7 of our wordlists?

_____

b. How is the _-ey_ pronounced when the accent is on some other syllable?

_____

c. Write in a homonym for each of the following words, being sure you know what the differences in meaning are:

     bey   grey   prey   trey

_____

5. A good word with which to begin your column of exceptions is _bass._ It has a homograph which is the name of a fish. Other common exceptions belong to a rhyming group; how many words can you write here which rhyme with _change?_

_____

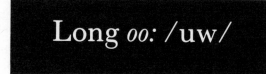

28

Long *oo* is generally made by /u/ followed by a *w*-glide. Some students have trouble distinguishing between /u/ and /uw/ at first. If you do, find someone who does not, and get him to repeat the word *root* to you, first as an old-time New England farmer would say it, with /u/ to rhyme with *put,* then as a city dweller would probably say it, with /uw/ to rhyme with *boot.* Have him do this until you too can reproduce both pronunciations. /uw/ is also readily confused with long *u,* which we take up next time; many dialects will use /uw/ where others use long *u,* and vice versa. In making out our wordlists we have followed the pronunciation given in *Webster's New Collegiate Dictionary,* but you may wish to change some words from one lesson to another, depending on the dialect you speak.

In written representation, /uw/ has the usual pattern, though it may be difficult to see at first. It also has one phonogram of foreign origin, and some specially exceptional phonograms designed to cause trouble for spellers.

Exercises

1	2	3	4
food	soup	blew	ruin
troop	troupe	yew	fluid
gloom	youth	crew	cruel
balloon	group	chew	frugal
caboose		shrewd	brutal
			crucial
booster		eschew	
moody		unscrew	juvenile
rootlet		crewel	fluency
schooner			plutocrat
cartoonist			pluperfect
harpooner			glutinous
booby	bouquet		intrusion
booty	coupon		exclusive
poodle	routine		incongruous
			perusal
coo	you		
moo	bayou		gnu
too	caribou		jujitsu
woo			
zoo			
bamboo			
igloo			
shampoo			
taboo			
tattoo			

5	6	7	8
rude	blue	do	
plume	flue	to	
fluke	rue	two	
truce		who	
rule	accrue	lose	
	construe	move	
exclude	imbrue	prove	
include	misconstrue	tomb	
recluse		womb	
parachute			
		bruise	
		bruit	
		cruise	
		fruit	
		juice	
		recruit	
		sluice	

1. After inspecting the wordlists carefully, answer the following questions:

   a. What is the usual spelling for /uw/ at the end of syllables other than final syllables?

   _____

   b. What phonograms are most commonly used at the end of a word?

   _____

   (Our wordlists have tried to suggest the approximate proportion of one phonogram to another except in column 7, where the two lists are relatively complete.)

   c. Look up the etymology of the words in column 2; what is the common national origin of most of these words?

   _____

   d. Disregarding columns 2 and 7, then, what phonograms are most commonly used to represent /uw/ in syllables ending in a consonant at the end of a word?

   _____

   e. In answering question d., could you see any distinction made between one-syllable words and longer ones?

   _____

   f. The words in column 7 (and their compounds and derivatives too, of course) must be learned as demons. Don't just look at them and assume that you know them; two words in the first group hold prominent positions in the list of most commonly misspelled words to be found in the final Review Lesson. Write below the difference between *to* and *lose* and their homonyms or near-homonyms:

   _____

   _____

2. In columns 3, 4, 5, and 6, one or the other of two sounds precedes /uw/ a great majority of the time. What are these two sounds? Remember them for the next lesson by writing them here:

_____

3. A majority of the polysyllabic words which could go in column 5 are derivatives of only two Latin verbs. Below, in our usual fashion, we give you the key Latin forms, the way they appear in English, and blank spaces for you to fill with examples:

cludere, clusus   clude, clus(e) _____

_____

trudere, trusus   trude, trus(e) _____

_____

You may find it convenient at this point to review exercise 4 in Chapter 20, which is concerned with /uw/ also.

29

Long *u:* /iw/, /ɨw/

Long *u* is made up of either /i/ or /ɨ/ followed by a *w*-glide, resulting in a vowel nucleus that has in the past often been described as consonantal /y/ followed by long *oo*. The presence of this /i/ element in long *u*, incidentally, should not lead you to insert a *y* where one does not belong. As we said last time, /uw/ and long *u* seem to be interchanged from one dialect to another; it is apparently very easy to substitute /i/ or /ɨ/ for /u/, or vice versa. The consonant sound preceding has some influence on which long vowel follows, as you saw last time: at one extreme are /č/, /ǰ/, /l/, /r/, after which /uw/ is much more prevalent; at the other extreme are /b/, /f/, /h/, /k/, /m/, /p/, and /v/, which generally tend to precede long *u*. The other consonants vary greatly even within one dialect, or within one speaker's usage.

In spelling, long *u* follows the usual pattern, with the addition of one foreign phonogram and a few special demons. Many of the phonograms are the same as those we have just been studying.

Exercises

1	2	3	4
curio	feud	few	cube
cubic	feudal	hew	fuse
bugle	deuce	view	huge
music	sleuth	ewe	pure
usage		newt	dispute
unit		lewd	misuse
unicorn	eugenics		perfume
mutiny	euphemism		execute
abusive	euphony	askew	molecule
impecunious	neurotic	curfew	ridicule
	neuter	nephew	vestibule
	pneumonia	review	photogravure
emu			
menu		ewer	
impromptu		newel	
		pewter	
		steward	

5	6	7
cue hue argue imbue rescue revue statue curlicue	suit nuisance pursuit	

1. After inspecting the wordlists, answer the following questions:

   a. What is the usual spelling for long *u* at the end of syllables other than final syllables?

   _____

   b. What phonograms are most commonly used for long *u* at the end of a word? (Once again our wordlists have tried to suggest the approximate proportions in this respect.)

   _____

   _____

   c. Look up the etymology of the words in the second group in column 2; the vast majority of words using this phonogram for long *u* have this same national origin—what is it?

   _____

   _____

(The first group of words in column 2 is an exception to your generalization about national origin; you may be interested in the origins of these words, so look them up also.)

   d. Disregarding column 2 temporarily, then, what phonogram is most commonly used to represent long *u* in syllables ending in a consonant at the end of a word?

   _____

   e. In answering question d., could you see any distinction made between one-syllable words and longer ones?

   _____

   _____

   _____

   f. *Webster's New Collegiate Dictionary* gives long *u* as the preferred pronunciation of *ui* in the words in column 6, but many persons employ /uw/ instead, as in the words in column 7 of the preceding lesson. What sound do *you* give it?

   _____

2. In our preliminary remarks this time we commented on the sounds which usually precede either long *u* or /uw/. According to *Webster's New Collegiate Dictionary,* the following pairs of words

are what the linguists call minimal pairs; they differ, in these pairs, in that one word has a long *u* where the other has /uw/. If these words form minimal pairs in your speech too, leave them alone, but if they make homonyms (i.e. are pronounced alike), draw a circle around that pair:

beauty	cue	feud	hew	mew
booty	coo	food	who	moo

pure	lute	due	tutor	suit
poor	loot	do	tooter	soot
				(secondary pron.)

In these minimal pairs, what do you notice about the phonograms which represent /uw/?

_____

_____

_____

30

Special Nucleus
oi: /oy/, /əy/

The commonest vowel nucleus heard for *oi* spellings today is the /o/ of *gonna* followed by a *y*-glide. Back in the eighteenth century the spelling *oi* was usually pronounced as long *i*, a pronunciation which still persists in some rural areas in the pronunciation of *boil* as /bayl/ and *join* as /jayn/, and quite generally in the pronunciation of *roil* as /rayl/ (sometimes even spelled *rile*). Somewhat the converse of this is the use in Ireland and a few Eastern Seaboard American dialects of /ɔ/ followed by a *y*-glide for sounds which in most dialects today are long *i*. (Have you ever heard a good raconteur tell a story in an Irish dialect, involving such words as *time* and *life*?) Finally, /ə/ followed by a *y*-glide produces the sound usually associated with certain New York City pronunciations of *first*, *bird*, and *shirt*, although the same phenomenon occurs in some southern coastal dialects. Unless you happen to speak one of these dialects which uses an /oy/-like nucleus for the long *i* or /ər/ of other dialects, you are not likely to have trouble with this sound in spelling.

The sounds we take up now are sometimes referred to as the "special" vowels, as they are the only nuclei of the many we have not mentioned already which English spelling has recognized. Actually they are the same sort of vowel nucleus as the so-called long vowels which we have just been studying, but in spelling these special vowels have developed a shorter and simpler pattern—one that you will probably find much more pleasant to study!

Exercises

1	2	3
oil	boy	oyster
toil	coy	boycott
joint	alloy	gargoyle
hoist	annoy	hoyden
devoid	convoy	
exploit	employ	
poison	enjoy	
moisture	corduroy	
ointment	viceroy	
adenoid		
boisterous		
	coyly	
	deployment	
	employed	
	joyous	
	joyride	

(continued)

1	2	3
	annoyance clairvoyant flamboyant loyal royal voyage arroyo foyer	

1. What is the usual spelling for /oy/ at the end of a word?

_____

2. What is the usual spelling for /oy/ before consonants?

_____

3. Under what circumstances does *oy* represent /oy/ before a consonant?

_____

4. The third column is for exceptions, and we have made the list relatively complete; what makes these words irregular?

_____

5. What is the usual spelling for /oy/ before vowels? (Except for a very few unusual words, this means in actual practice, before easily recognized suffixes such as *-al, -ance, -ed, -ing, -ous,* and so on.)

_____

31

Special Nucleus
ou: /aw/, /æw/

The nucleus often represented by *ou* is made by either /æ/ or /a/ followed by a *w*-glide. The latter is preferred by teachers of speech, as the former is considered too nasal, but it is the more widespread. The spelling *ou* is in a few dialects sounded as /e/ followed by a *w*-glide, a nucleus nearer to long *o* than this nucleus, and one which we mentioned with long *o*.

The spelling of /aw/ does not follow the pattern of /oy/ too well, but its variations themselves form a pattern of their own, so that this sound should not cause the speller too much trouble.

Exercises

1	2	3	4
cloud	cow	fowl	plough
drouth	how	growl	bough
found	prow	howl	slough
house	scow	prowl	sough
ounce	vow	scowl	drought
foul	bow		doughty
our	plow		
out	allow	brown	
pouch	endow	down	
south	somehow	drown	
		town	
county	coward		thou
scoundrel	dowager	crowd	
mountain	endowment	dowdy	
devour	flower	powder	
pronounce	prowess		
account	rowen		sauerkraut
compound	rowan	browse	
paramount	towel	frowzy	
	trowel		
	vowel		

1. What is the usual spelling for /aw/ at the end of a word?

_____

2. What is the usual spelling for /aw/ before vowels?

_____

3. If /aw/ followed the pattern of /oy/ exactly, what phonogram would you expect to represent /aw/ before consonants?

_____

4. The phonogram *ow* appears for /aw/ before consonants more frequently than *oy* did for /oy/, but there is a little pattern even here. Answer the following questions about column 3 and you will see it:

   a. What homonym of a word in group 1 is the only exception (with its compounds and derivatives, of course) to the generalization that before *l* you always use *ow* for /aw/?

   _____

   b. The only exception to the generalization that before *n* alone (i.e. not followed by another consonant) you always use *ow* for /aw/ is the name of a part of speech. What is it?

   _____

   c. Before *d, crowd* is an exceptional one-syllable word (cf. *cloud, loud, proud, shroud*); the multi-syllabic words which use *ow* for /aw/ before *d* all rhyme with *dowdy* and *powder*. What are they?

   _____

   d. Before /z/, there is no good generalization, but eye-rhymes of *browse* and *frowzy* will give you most of the common examples of *ow*. You might also, at this time, review exercise 4c. in Chapter 15. Write out here all the examples you can find:

   _____

   e. What may appear to be exceptions before other consonants are often words in which a vowel following the *ow* has disappeared, as in *dowry*, originally *dowery*. Can you think of any other examples of this sort? Write them here:

   _____

5. Our old enemy *-ough* can also represent /aw/; in column 4 we have listed most of the examples. The commonest ones are developing alternative spellings that are more regular; write below any such that you know or discover, indicating with an asterisk those that are preferred spellings:

_____

_____

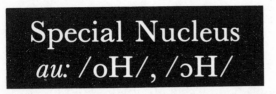

32

Special Nucleus
au: /oH/, /ɔH/

The vowel nucleus often represented by *au* is made with either the /o/ of *gonna* or /ɔ/ followed by an /H/-glide. The resulting sound is very hard for many persons to distinguish from /ɔ/ itself, and at times when one sound is used the other can easily be substituted. As we never *hear* accurately the sounds we ourselves make, either find someone who can distinguish the sounds for you, or feel in your mouth the difference in creating them: say the word *talk,* allowing the point at which the vowel is made to remain steadily at one place in the back of your mouth; this is /ɔ/. Then say the word again, allowing the point at which the vowel sound is made to rise slowly toward the top of the mouth before being shut off by the /k/ sound; this is /oH/ or /ɔH/.

We have already seen in Chapter 8 that /ɔ/ is frequently an allophone of /a/; it is also at times an allophone of /oH/. In fact, depending on the emphasis in the sentence and the emotional intensity of the speaker, the pronunciation of the same word may vary from /ɔ/ to /oH/. As an allophone of /oH/, /ɔ/ is represented by the same phonograms as /oH/. The speller's real problem with /ɔ/ is to decide which set of phonograms to use for any particular appearance of it—those for /a/ or those for /oH/. The nucleus /oH/ has phonograms which follow the pattern of /oy/ and /aw/, but the general situation is complicated by three different sounds which change an adjoining vowel to /oH/. Look at the wordlists carefully, and then do the exercises.

Exercises

1	2	3	4	5	6
daub	claw	gawk	all	cord	aught
cause	saw	hawk	ball	scorch	caught
fault	squaw	squawk	call	absorb	distraught
haul	guffaw	awkward	chalk	border	fraught
maul	outlaw	mawkish	talk	corner	naught
taut	oversaw		walk	escort	onslaught
applause	withdraw		salt	order	taught
bauble		bawl	alter	abnormal	daughter
caution		brawl	already	porcupine	slaughter
faucet		crawl			
fauna		scrawl			
sausage		yawl			
binaural					
cauliflower					
nautical					
tarpaulin					
tautology					

(continued)

1	2	3	4	5	6
	awful	brawn	dwarf		bought
	drawer	fawn	thwart		brought
	flawless	lawn	walnut		fought
	hawthorn	spawn	want		nought
	lawful	yawn	warble		ought
	lawyer	tawny	warm		sought
	rawest	awning	warp		thought
	sawing		wash		wrought
	strawy		water		
	withdrawal	bawd			awe
		tawdry			hawser
		dawdle			
					broad

1. What is the usual spelling for /oH/ at the end of a word?

_____

2. What is the usual spelling for /oH/ before vowels?

_____

3. There are two conditions, under either of which *a* may represent /oH/. Fill in the spaces below with your statements as to what these conditions are:

    a. _____

    b. _____

4. Look at the pronunciations given in your dictionary for all the words beginning with *al-* and *wa-*. Does *a* always represent /oH/ under the circumstances you mentioned in your answer to question 3, or just may it?

_____

5. For a great many people, *o* before /r/ becomes /oH/. The dictionary, for example, gives /oH/ (or whatever its symbol for the nucleus is—often ô) as the proper vowel sound to go in the word *cord*. Others hear a long *o* sound here. People are apparently inconsistent even with themselves, for the dictionary lists long *o* as the proper pronunciation for *ford*. If you hear /oH/ in the words in column 5, be prepared to spell the nucleus with an *o* before /r/. Exceptions are discussed below:

    a. The phonogram *au* appears before /r/ in only a handful of words, all derived from even fewer Latin roots. Look up the etymologies of the following words and list under them any others from the same root which you can find and think might be useful:

        laurel   minotaur   aural   aura

_____

_____

_____

b. Review exercise 7 in Review Lesson 7. Why does an *o* never sound /oH/ before /r/ and after /w/?

_____

_____

c. How do you spell /oH/ after /w/ and before /r/? (See column 4 of today's wordlists for the answer.)

_____

_____

d. The phonogram *aw* for /oH/ never precedes /r/, though it may seem to if an intervening vowel is slighted, as in *drawer*. Can you add here any other similar words?

_____

6. If we accept the pattern of /oy/ as the standard for the vowel nuclei we have been studying this week, we would expect the phonogram *au* to appear before consonants. But a glance at column 3 will suggest that the pattern for /oH/ is closer to that of /aw/ than to that of /oy/. The following exercises may help you to straighten all this out:

a. Before /n/, /oH/ is quite regular and behaves exactly as does /aw/. Write out here your generalization on how to spell /oH/ before /n/:

_____

_____

b. In one-syllable words in which the /l/ is final, the phonogram *aw* is very common preceding the /l/. Many of these words have homonyms ending in *-all*. Make a list here of words with these phonograms, learning now how to distinguish between the homonyms. The words will fall into two eye-rhyme families which we have begun for you:

bawl _____

ball _____

c. In one-syllable words when the /l/ is followed by another consonant, or in non-final syllables of multisyllabic words, *a* is the commonest phonogram for /oH/ before /l/.

d. About a dozen very common exceptions to b. and c. are provided by the phonogram *au;* we have listed a few of them in column 1. Eye as well as ear rhymes of some of them should suggest other examples to you. Write any other examples of *au* before *l* here:

_____

e. Before /k/, the field is about evenly divided between *aw* and *a* (Is the silent *l* a part of a vowel digraph, or part of a fossil blend of consonants? Review exercise 1 in Chapter 10.) in final syllables, whether of one-syllable or multisyllabic words. The one exception, which uses *au,* is the name of a bird popular in crossword puzzles. What is it?

_____

f. In the earlier syllables of longer words (compounds and derivatives of words covered by e. do not count, of course) *au* is the usual phonogram, as in *caucus, raucous,* and *auction.* (Notice that *au* usually appears before a *c* rather than a *k* in this type of word.) Can you add any words to this list?

g. The phonogram *aw* appears for /oH/ before /d/ only irregularly. The compounds and derivatives of the examples given in column 3 will provide you with all the common words using *aw* before *d*. Can you add any others here?

h. A few of the words in column 2, the second group, may seem to be exceptions to some of the things we have just been saying (*flawless, hawthorn,* and *lawful,* for example). Why are these not exceptions?

7. The phonograms *-augh* and *-ough* are also used for /oH/ in a handful of words each. Except for compounds and derivatives, and very unusual or uncommon words, our lists in column 6 are relatively complete.

a. Do you notice anything about the limited circumstances in which these phonograms are used?

b. The only one-syllable word using *au* in this same way is a homonym for one of the words using *augh*. Write the two homonyms below and be sure you know what each one means:

c. Longer words using *au* before *t* are all derived from a few Greek roots. We illustrate the two commonest below; how many more words from these roots can you find that you think will be useful? Write them in:

tautology   argonaut

8. Now review the exercises in Chapter 8.

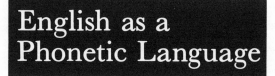

English as a Phonetic Language

One of the commonest excuses offered for the prevalence of bad spelling today is the idea that English is not a phonetic language. That is perhaps putting the cart before the horse. English *is* a phonetic language; every language which uses an alphabet or other set of phonetic symbols is phonetic. But the history of the English language has been one of continual change, and as these changes often affect you as a speller of modern English, we propose to give you a very brief history of the language, emphasizing and illustrating most fully those changes which concern you most.

English is a member of a large family of languages known as the Indo-European languages. They share certain peculiarities unknown to other languages outside the group, the most important probably being the system of *inflection,* that is, the change or variation in the form of a word to show its relationship to other words. This is a broad definition, and this type of inflection may conveniently be broken down into two parts: (1) the use of inflectional endings or changes to indicate such grammatical concepts as person (*I sing, he sings*), number (*cat, cats*), case (*he, him*), gender (*he, she, it;* no really good example still exists in modern English), tense (*walk, walked*); and (2) compounding, or putting together of two word elements, each of which has a more or less independent existence; the degrees of this independence may vary from a compound word such as *blackbird* or *roommate,* to the addition of a suffix to indicate a part of speech, as *swiftly* and *stubbornness.* Secondly, the Indo-European languages seem to share a common basic vocabulary, with words quite different from those for the same objects, acts, and so on, in other groups of languages.

The Indo-European languages may further be subdivided into eight groups, some of which are fairly large. English belongs to the group known as Teutonic, which includes ancient Gothic, modern German, the Scandinavian languages, Dutch, Frisian, and others. This group is distinguished from other Indo-European languages by certain differences in consonant sounds which are quite regular and were first categorized by a German linguist, Jacob Grimm, in 1822. According to Grimm's Law (i.e. Grimm's generalizations about what he saw in the languages), the original Indo-European /p/ became Teutonic /f/, /t/ became /θ/, and /k/ became /h/, as in Latin *pater,* English *father;* Latin *piscis,* English *fish;* Latin *tres,* English *three;* Latin *cornus,* English *horn;* Greek ποδος (podos), Latin *pes, pedis,* English *foot.* In other words, the voiceless aspirated stops /p, t, k/ became the corresponding voiceless slit spirants /f, θ, h/ (see chart on p. 132). In other changes, the voiced aspirated stops /b, d, g/ became the voiceless aspirated stops /p, t, k/ respectively, and the aspirates /bh, dh, gh/ became the voiced aspirated stops /b, d, g/. For example, Latin *decem,* English *ten;* Sanskrit *bharāmi,* English *bear.* This last change explains, of course, why these aspirates are no longer separate phonemes in English.

The Teutonic languages are further characterized by (1) the classification of verbs as strong (or irregular; for example, *sing, sang, sung*) and weak (or regular; for example, *talk, talked, talked*); (2) the twofold declension of adjectives as strong and weak, which we will illustrate later, but which has disappeared entirely in modern English; and (3) the Teutonic system of *fixed* accent—that is, the accent in native or naturalized words is almost always on the first syllable of the word, or at least on the first syllable of the root. This still holds in English; a noun or verb keeps the same accent usually through all its various inflections. Latin, on the contrary, which represents the *free* accent of the non-Teutonic Indo-European languages, changes the accent with various forms of the word: cf. Latin *imperátor, imperatórem,* and English *émperor*. This accent is important in spelling, but will cause less trouble in Teutonic roots than in Latinate and other borrowed words, where the accent is still unstable at times.

The history of English as a distinct Teutonic language may be said to begin about 449 A.D., the traditional date for the arrival of the first contingent of Angles, Saxons, and Jutes in what is now known as England (Angle-land). England, or Britain as it had been known, was previously inhabited by people speaking different languages of the Celtic branch of the Indo-European family. For roughly four hundred years many of these people had been under the rule of the Romans, and had been protected and civilized by them. But when, about 410 A.D., the Romans withdrew their last forces, the untrained native population (although of Celtic stock for the most part, they thought of themselves as Romans, of course) was left at the mercy of the related but wilder and more uncivilized tribes who had never been subjugated by the Romans and who had been harassing the Britons with raids for some time. According to legend, the former Roman subjects sought aid from the Angles, Saxons, and Jutes, and those who came to help stayed to conquer. In any event, it took the newcomers little more than a century to drive the Celts back up into Scotland, where 150,000 people still speak Gaelic, west into the mountains of Wales, where a Celtic language spoken by over two million people still flourishes, southwest into Cornwall, where a Celtic language survived until the eighteenth century, and across the Channel into Brittany, the northwestern corner of France, where many people still speak a Celtic tongue, Breton.

Although the earliest written records of Anglo-Saxon or Old English preserved date from about the seventh century, from them it is abundantly clear that these immigrants from the North Sea coastal areas of what are now Germany and Denmark brought with them a language highly inflected in comparison with modern English, and very limited in vocabulary. The noun, for example, was declined for four cases in both singular and plural. There were two main declensions of nouns, each subdivided into several classes. Gender was grammatical, not natural as it is today. Every adjective had to agree with the noun it modified in number, case, and gender. It could do this in two ways; after a definite article or a demonstrative pronoun it took what is known as a *weak* form, and when it stood alone it was declined in the *strong* form. For example, "these young boys" would be translated *þas geongan cnapan,* but "young boys" would be *geonge cnapan.* Other examples could be given from the verbs, adverbs, and pronouns to show how much more complicated the system of inflection was in the Old English period, but this will perhaps suffice to suggest to you that one reason why we have trouble at times with inflectional endings is that we have grown so accustomed to doing without them except in a few places, that we tend to forget even the few that are left.

When the Anglo-Saxons came to their new home, they probably brought with them their old runic alphabet, but by the time our records begin it had been largely replaced by the Latin one. Only five runic letters remained: eth (ð) and thorn (þ), for the voiced and voiceless sounds of *th* (though even when the preserved written records begin the two phonograms seem to be used interchangeably); wen (ᚹ) for /w/; the digraph which we use in our phonetic alphabet for the simple or short *a,* /æ/, represented the same sound in Old English; and finally *g* was represented in at least some of its uses by ȝ. Our table of consonants shows that, as today, there were 24 consonant sounds. Although we use the same phonetic symbols, these were not necessarily always exactly the same as the corresponding ones today, having been made a little bit farther forward in the mouth in some cases, or a little bit farther back in others. One sound, /ž/ had not yet been introduced, and another, the voiced counterpart of /h/, which we represent by /x/, has disappeared in modern English. This last sound, pronounced like the final consonant in the Scots *loch*, was usually written *h*, as in *þurh* (modern *through*).

These 24 consonant sounds had to be represented by 17 letters, so that from the very beginning English has not had enough single symbols to go around and has had to use digraphs or make letters represent more than one sound. As today, *c, g,* and *s* were the ones which did the most double duty. The letter *c* represented /k/ most commonly, as in *cēne* (*bold*); it also represented /č/ as in *cirice* (*church*). This latter use was primarily before the front vowels /i/ and /e/. The letter also served as part of various digraphs: in *cg* to represent /ǰ/ as in *brycg* (*bridge*), and in *sc* to represent /š/, as in *scip* (*ship*). The letter *g* or its runic counterpart, ȝ, represented three sounds by itself: its modern sound /g/, as in *glæd* (*glad*); /y/ as in *geard* (*yard*); and rarely /ǰ/ as in *sengan* (*singe*). The voiceless spirants /f/, /θ/, and /s/ became voiced when standing between vowels or between *r* or *l* and a vowel, as in *drifan* (*drive*) and *freosan* (*freeze*), but with no change in spelling; hence /v/ and /z/ were represented by *f* and *s* respectively, and *þ* became the commoner representative of the two middle slit spirants. The sound /ŋ/ was represented by *n* and occurred only before /g/ and /k/. The following /g/ was always pronounced in Old English, as it is today in *finger*, but is not in *singer*. The voiceless aspirated stops (/p, t, k/) were often doubled before /r/ and /l/, as in *bitter* (*bitter*), *æppel* (*apple*), *miccle* (*great*), and occasionally their voiced counterparts were too, as in *næddre* (*serpent, adder*), thus creating the third largest group of double letters in English.

Table VI. Consonant Sounds of Early Old English,
with Their Commonest Phonograms in Parentheses

	Front	Middle	Back
Stops			
Aspirated			
voiced	/b/ (*b*)	/d/ (*d*)	/g/ (*g*, ȝ)
voiceless	/p/ (*p*)	/t/ (*t*)	/k/ (*c*)
Affricated			
voiced		/ǰ/ (*cg, g*)	
voiceless		/č/ (*c*)	
Spirants			
Slit			
voiced	/v/ (*f*)	/ð/ (*þ, ð*)	/x/ (*h*)
voiceless	/f/ (*f*)	/θ/ (*þ, ð*)	/h/ (*h*)
Grooved			
voiced		/z/ (*s*)	
voiceless		/s/ (*s*)	/š/ (*sc*)
Resonants			
Lateral, voiced		/l/ (*l*)	
Nasal, voiced	/m/ (*m*)	/n/ (*n*)	/ŋ/ (*n*)
Median, voiced	/w/ (ƿ)	/r/ (*r*)	/y/ (*g*)

The vowels form a very rough approximation of our present system also. The short, or simple vowels were /æ, e, i, ɔ, a, u/ with the other three being dialectal additions or variations. /æ, e, i, a, u/ were represented in Old English by their present phonetic symbols, and /ɔ/ by o. The complex vowels are a bit more complicated. /aH/ was represented by $\bar{a}$ (the diacritical mark to indicate length was not used in the old manuscripts, of course, but it is customary to indicate length in modern editions of the ancient texts); /ey/ by $\bar{e}$, /iy/ by $\bar{i}$, /ow/ by $\bar{o}$, /uw/ by $\bar{u}$, and /uy/ (not a common nucleus in modern English) by $\bar{y}$. In addition to these six long vowels, Old English had three common diphthongs, ea, eo, and ie, in which the first vowel could be either long or short, thus making really six diphthongs.

The breakdown of the Old English inflectional system began about the tenth century, and is still going on (consider what is happening to the apostrophe in the possessive case). In the first place, there was no great literature in the language, either in quality or in quantity, to be revered and thus serve as a conservative force as it did, for example, in Latin. The arts of reading and writing were not widespread, and there were few schools and few teachers to serve as another conserving force. And finally, in the eighth century the Anglo-Saxons were themselves subjected to the same kind of treatment they had given to the Celts; they were invaded by the Danes, and after almost a century of fighting had been driven out of most of the northeastern third of England. A long period of warfare of this sort will produce social and political unrest enough to allow a language to develop in an untrammeled and popular way. Another theory is that once they stopped fighting and learned to live peaceably together, the two groups realized that they spoke very similar languages, words often having the same root and differing only in inflectional ending. Thus, the conjecture is, they were led to drop the endings in order to understand one another better. Whatever the reason, the speakers of Old English certainly began to pronounce their inflectional endings less carefully, perhaps giving more accent to the root than before, and even less to the ending, which had always been unaccented.

In addition to beginning the degeneration of inflectional endings, the Old Norse language spoken by the Danish invaders left one or two permanent marks on English spelling. Although the Danes still used a completely runic alphabet, they may well have encouraged the introduction of the letter k from the continent at this time. As sc customarily represented /š/, Old English had no way of representing the combination /sk/, yet at this time it was borrowing a number of words such as skin (from Old Norse skinn) which had this combination. And it was about the time of the invasions of the Danes or a little later that the old manuscripts begin to use k before e and i. Although the introduction of k may have been designed primarily to alleviate some of the confusion caused by having c represent both /k/ and /č/, it did not always succeed, as the modern words shirt and skirt testify. Skirt is derived from the Old Norse word skyrta, which meant "shirt"; shirt is descended from Old English scyrte (pronounced /širte/), meaning "skirt"!

The tendency to drop inflections was furthered by the Norman invasion of 1066, which made the dominant language in England a dialect of French and again allowed English to develop in an uninhibited and popular manner. Various non-linguistic causes helped in the revival of English as the dominant language of England after three hundred years of being the language of serfs. As long as they could go back and forth between Normandy and England easily, the Anglo-Norman aristocracy got along very well without the English language. But early in the thirteenth century French military successes, and a decree by the French king that no one could hold both an English and a French title and lands, tended to cut them off from France. Then the Plague, respecting no particular language, appeared in the fourteenth century, and made the need for Englishmen in every walk of life acute. Ultimately, by 1400 English was again the language in general use. During the period since 1066, however, the old inflectional system of the Teutonic language had almost completely broken down.

The Old English vocabulary, which had been slender, was enriched by the addition of many new words from French, especially during the fourteenth century, when the social barriers between Norman and English were rapidly breaking down and Englishmen were first able to aspire to high positions. The French spoken by Englishmen was laughed at on the Continent (those of you who have read the Prologue to the *Canterbury Tales* will remember Chaucer's gentle joke about the Prioress, who spoke the French of "Stratford atte Bowe" for the French of Paris was unknown to her[1]); yet enough prestige clung to this language of the upper classes to make the English want to lard their language with French words. The same linguistic phenomenon is observable today, though on a much smaller scale, in our use of *fiancee, foyer, debutante,* and other words which have a synonym already established in the language but lacking in the distinction words are felt to receive from the French.

Perhaps of most interest to modern students of spelling, however, are the new phonograms introduced into the language by the Norman scribes (who were for many years almost the only people in England able to write), struggling to deal with a strange language and strange phonograms. The most important were those replacing the old runic symbols. The digraph æ was replaced by *a,* and the wen (Þ) by *w*—this last being one of the first changes to occur. /g/ came to be represented by the Roman *g,* and *g*'s /y/ sound ultimately became *y,* although ȝ survived in handwriting down to the end of the period. One phonogram, *th,* replaced both the eth (ð) and the thorn (þ) late in the Middle English Period (1100–1500); earlier *th* was used only in learned words and proper names, and was pronounced /t/ as in *Thomas,* and, as we have noted, þ became the popular symbol for both these runic phonograms. But the introduction of printing into England in the 1470's put an end to the use of these distinctive phonograms, as all the type used in England was for some time made on the continent where these symbols were not used.

Several other phonograms were introduced by Norman scribes as being more familiar than some of the symbols used in the English manuscripts they were copying. For example, in Old English *cg* represented /ǰ/; the Norman scribes introduced the letter *j* to take its place. The Old English *cw* in the same fashion became *qu,* /uw/ became *ou* (pronounced much as in modern French, not modern English), and *sc* became *sh.* And through borrowings from French which already had the sounds /v/ or /z/ represented by *v* or *z,* these two new phonograms for the voiced spirants were introduced into English. The phonogram *ph,* which, like *th,* was also used mainly in learned words (primarily Latin borrowings from Greek which had then come down into French) and proper names, was first introduced at this time. /č/, being close to the sound represented by *ch* in French, took over this phonogram. *C,* however, took on a new sound, beginning at this time to represent /s/ in words borrowed from French, as *face.* In other borrowings from French, /ž/ first appeared, as in *azure.* And the voiced back slit spirant /x/ was finally represented by *gh* (Old English *dohtor* became *doghtor,* modern *daughter*).

---

[1] For other contemporary references to the poor quality of French spoken in England, see Albert C. Baugh, *A History of the English Language,* 2nd ed., New York, Appleton-Century-Crofts, 1957, pp. 167–8.

Table VII. Consonant Sounds of Middle English c. 1400, with Their Commonest Phonograms in Parentheses

	Front		Middle		Back	
Stops						
Aspirated						
voiced	/b/	(b)	/d/	(d)	/g/	(g)
voiceless	/p/	(p)	/t/	(t)	/k/	(c, k)
Affricated						
voiced			/ǰ/	(j, cg)		
voiceless			/č/	(ch)		
Spirants						
Slit						
voiced	/v/	(f, v)	/ð/	(þ, th)	/x/	(gh)
voiceless	/f/	(f, ph)	/θ/	(þ, th)	/h/	(h)
Grooved						
voiced			/z/	(s, z)	/ž/	(z)
voiceless			/s/	(s, c)	/š/	(sh)
Resonants						
Lateral, voiced			/l/	(l)		
Nasal, voiced	/m/	(m)	/n/	(n)	/ŋ/	(n)
Median, voiced	/w/	(w)	/r/	(r)	/y/	(y, ʒ)

The re-establishment of English as the dominant language did not mean the end of change, however. The fifteenth century was another period of political and social unrest, marked by the last half of the Hundred Years War, and the long-drawn-out civil strife known as the War of the Roses. During this century what is known as the Great Vowel Shift in English was completed; although parts of it at least may have had their beginnings much earlier, the major portion of the change took place during this century. While all vowel sounds may have been changing somewhat, the most important changes were in the long vowels, as follows:

$$/aH/ \rightarrow /ow/ \qquad (hām \rightarrow home)$$
$$/ow/ \rightarrow /uw/ \qquad (mōd \rightarrow mood)$$
$$/uw/ \rightarrow /aw/ \qquad (hūs \rightarrow house)$$
$$/ey/ \rightarrow /iy/ \qquad (slēpan \rightarrow sleep)$$
$$/iy/ \rightarrow /ay/ \qquad (hwīt \rightarrow white)$$

In other words, each vowel moved forward a little in position, and the spelling adapted itself to the new sounds. This left the single letters *a* and *e* not representing long vowels, and the sounds /aH/ and /ey/ vacant. This situation was taken care of by new borrowings, and, more importantly, by other vowel changes in English itself. At this same time, the short vowels except /i/ and /u/ were lengthened before a single consonant followed by a weak or unaccented vowel. In this way, for example, Old English *nama* became *name,* the *a* having the sound of the continental long *e*. Later, in very early modern English, when all the inflectional vowel endings had been leveled to *-e,* the letter was retained even when it was no longer pronounced when it would distinguish between two potential homonyms, as *hate* and *hat,* or *hope* and *hop,* and thus the final silent *e* came to be regarded as a sign of length in the preceding vowel, as it is today.

With the beginning of modern English, grammatical changes ceased to be so great, but sound changes and additions to the vocabulary kept on. It is these two, in fact, that are largely responsible for much of the speller's woe today. As early as the first part of the

Modern English Period (i.e. 1500–1600), there was a strong feeling that a standardized spelling would be desirable. Most individuals kept their own spelling fairly consistent, but there was great variation from one person to another in spite of the standardizing influence of a number of spelling reformers and, not least, of the printers. During this century "long" or double consonants were shortened, and came to be pronounced as they are today, like single consonants. But as the double letter showed that the preceding vowel was short, the spelling was retained, and the doubling extended to many letters not previously doubled: *penny, copper, herring,* for example. Unfortunately this doubling was not carried out too consistently, and we have modern *rabbit* and *habit* (which rhyme) coming from Middle English *rabett* and *habit*. As the letters *u* and *v* were used interchangeably, it became customary to keep the silent *e* after *v* even when the vowel was short, to avoid confusion (*lou* or *lov* could otherwise be interpreted as either *love* or *low*).

During the seventeenth century a further weakening of some sounds occurred: /w/ was dropped (in pronunciation) in unaccented syllables, as in *towards,* and became silent before /r/ as in *write;* /t/ preceded by /s/ or /f/ and followed by /l/, /m/, or /n/ became silent, as in *thistle, Christmas, often, chestnut.*

By the eighteenth century, gradual but steady changes in sound and the influence of printers had created an atmosphere receptive to a standardization of spelling. Early in the century Swift proposed an Academy to "fix" the language, i.e. to stabilize it and keep it from changing. The poets Mark Akenside and Thomas Edwards and others proposed spelling reforms. But it took the authority and prestige of Dr. Johnson's famous *Dictionary* (1755) to standardize English spelling for the first time. Except for a few American variations on British usage, proposed by Noah Webster in his spelling books and dictionary, our spelling follows essentially the pattern set up by Dr. Johnson over two hundred years ago.

But the language has gone on changing in sound and adding new words in these two centuries. Anyone who reads much of the poetry of Alexander Pope (1688–1744) will notice rhymes which were true in his day but are false today (familiar examples are *tea* and *obey,* and *join* and *divine*). And the increase in our scientific learning and our knowledge of the world in general has led to the coining of many new technical terms based mainly on Latin and Greek roots, and to increased borrowings from many different languages. In these more recent borrowings the tendency has been to preserve the original spelling, thus bringing into English many new and unnecessary phonograms. This has made some knowledge of the etymology of words, and an understanding of the proper way to use a dictionary, essential to a modern speller.

Fortunately the answer to this complexity lies in what too many students try to employ without knowing how—phonetic spelling. The newspapers recently carried an account of a young soldier whose report of an adventure illustrates what untutored phonetic spelling can be like:

> I . . . will on duddy on the 20 Sept 1957 at approx 2255 I was walking post 6 witch is loketed on the south side of the matence hanger at the south end of the parkind airia. I was woking est by the wase of the paved ramp at approx the senter of the parkind airia when a radil snack sounded his worning I druw my weppen and fired.[2]

This passage illustrates a number of things. It shows how badly one can misspell and still be understood. Spelling, as long as it "approxes" the sound, does not have to be "correct"

---

[2] *New York Herald Tribune,* Sept. 6, 1959, Section 1, p. 18.

so far as communication is concerned—except that this young soldier was communicating a lot about himself that was not contained in the denotations of his words. It also shows how badly many people associate sound with symbol; we trust you were duly horrified to see *dd* and *ck* following a long vowel. Even worse, however, is the obvious failure to hear or be aware of the sounds one is using. Unless his speech was more slovenly than most, he was not hearing in "matence" all the sounds he was using. And the use of *will* for (presumably) *went* indicates further lack of consciousness of the sounds he is representing.

We hope that from working with this book you have gained some insight into the phonetic structure of English, and the way the language represents its sounds in writing. We hope we have been able to stretch the size of your vocabulary also. And perhaps most of all, we hope we have made you conscious of language and how it works, and more aware of words and diction. As we said in the introduction, we don't anticipate that you'll never "get set," but we do hope you have sharpened your linguistic game enough so that you can even pull off a grand slam occasionally!

Review Lesson I: for Chapters 1-4

1. Without looking back, see whether or not you can fill in the correct phonetic symbols for the nine simple vowels in the proper spaces below:

	front	middle	back
high			
middle			
low			

2. Can you, without looking back, fill in the phonetic symbols for the eight stops in the proper spaces below?

		front	middle	back
aspirates:	voiced			
	voiceless			
affricates:	voiced			
	voiceless			

3. Do the same for the spirants:

		front	middle	back
slit:	voiced			
	voiceless			
grooved:	voiced			
	voiceless			

4. And then similarly with the resonants:

		front	middle	back
lateral:	voiced			
	voiceless			
nasal:	voiced			
	voiceless			
median:	voiced			
	voiceless			

5. Give a definition in your own words, and an illustration, of the following terms:

phoneme _____

_____

stop _____

_____

resonant _____

_____

syllabic _____

_____

derivative _____

_____

phonogram _____

_____

minimal pair _____

_____

aspiration _____

_____

affricate _____

_____

spirant _____

_____

nasal _____

_____

vowel nucleus _____

_____

voice (voiced) _____

_____

accent _____

_____

assimilation _____

_____

6. To see how well you have understood the guides to syllabication, try to epitomize each one in one sentence, providing for all the subdivisions of each guide in your sentence:

(I) _____

(II) _____

(III) _____

(IV) _____

7. a. Suppose you are reading an old letter, in which the month of the date is written "7ber." In what month was the letter written, and where in your dictionary would you find out?

_____

b. Look up the entry under *phlegmatic* in your dictionary, and explain below all the abbreviations contained in it:

_____

_____

8. Reversals or transpositions were common in Old English as well as today. Although *wh* as a spelling for /hw/ is the only one which has succeeded in establishing itself universally, there are traces of others still. Look up the following words in an historical dictionary, and write in the early form of the word of which the modern word shows a reversal:

ask   crisp   run   third   through

_____

_____

_____

_____

9. After each of the following words write the word (or words) with which it is easily confused, and explain why they are confused (i.e. into what classification of homonym or near-homonym do they fit?):

strait _____

_____

brake _____

_____

chord _____

_____

cite _____

_____

waste _____

_____

whose _____

_____

you're _____

_____

10. What three blends can be either initial or final?

_____

_____

11. Before we even begin work on them, can you think of any fossil blends? List them, with illustrative words:

_____

_____

_____

12. Before you read the words in the following lists, get a friend to read them aloud to you, and see how many initial and final sounds you can record correctly. Remember, we are interested in the sounds, not the initial and final letters necessarily. Any plausible substitutions (*k* for hard *c,* for example) will be considered correct as long as it represents the sound clearly:

allomorph	matriculate	rhetoric	ustulation
wrist	whisk	them	oppugnancy
visiting	yaw	drogue	peccadillo
chattel	educe	harborage	cerebellum
winterize	beleaguer	spectrograph	shibboleth

13. The following syllables could all appear in English words. We have isolated them here, however, and want you to tell us whether the vowel you hear (every combination of letters is *one* syllable only) is long or short. Mark them with the proper diacritical marks—a line over the long vowels, and inverted semi-circle over the short ones:

zate	ded	pre	dain	bede
jite	cu	lat	foat	deud
tri	ject	ire	cred	vade

14. Is English spelling phonetic or not? Explain:

_____

_____

_____

_____

Review Lesson II: for Chapters 5-7

You are now completing your first group of lessons dealing with spelling generalizations; it is now time to consolidate what you have learned and make sure you have not missed anything. The following exercises are designed to make you do a number of things: apply your generalizations in various ways, make other generalizations based on those you have already made, and in general go back over the same material with different words and different types of exercises.

1. In Chapter 4 we gave you four generalizations based on generalizations. List below the numbers of those we have encountered so far. Then after each, give the lesson and number of an exercise which illustrates it:

_____

_____

2. Formulate below a phonic generalization which will cover the use of both *tch* and *dge* (You will find that that useful word *respectively* may be of assistance to you here.):

_____

_____

3. Among the following words are some which are perfectly regular, and some which you should have discovered as exceptions to your generalizations about *tch* and *dge* (see exercise 2 in chapters 5 and 6). Underline the exceptions:

college	subterfuge	knowledge	sandwich	rich
which	strange	porridge	partridge	such
detach	ostrich	cartridge	abridge	bewitch
much	charge	niche	privilege	touch

4. The number of suffixes creating real or apparent exceptions to your generalizations about *tch* and *dge* (see exercise 3 in Chapters 5 and 6) are few in number, and many of the words they cre-

ate are rare or uncommon. Below are examples of all the endings, with some of the commonest words which they create. Look up the etymologies of these words, and underline those which seem to be true exceptions to your generalizations:

bludgeon	cudgel	kitchen	badger	fidget
escutcheon	ratchet	dudgeon	satchel	crotchet

5. You have, we hope, concluded from exercises 8 and 10 in Chapter 6 that almost the only time that *j* appears before *e* or *i* in the middle of a word (it never appears before *y*) is when the Latin root *-jec* or *-ject* is used. With that fact in mind, underline below any words that seem to you to be exceptions to your phonic generalizations:

adjust	gyrate	ajar	adjective
congestion	majestic	energy	magic

6. a. Having done exercise 5 in Chapters 5 and 6, can you now formulate a phonic generalization as to when to expect the palatalization of /t/ and /d/ before long /u/? Write your generalization here:

_____

_____

b. When is this palatalization most likely to trouble you as a speller?

_____

_____

7. a. Can you write a generalization for the palatalization of /t/ before /i/ followed by /ə/ without looking back at exercise 6, Chapter 5? Write it here:

_____

_____

b. Can you write a similar generalization for /d/ before an /i/ followed by /ə/? Write it here:

_____

_____

8. A suffix may make one particular spelling at the end of a word extremely common, and influence unwary spellers to spell other similar endings of words incorrectly. An example is the suffix *-age*, pronounced /ĭj/; words with this suffix constitute the great majority of multisyllabic words ending in /j/ preceded by a short vowel, and explain why *college* and *privilege* are so often misspelled with an *-age* at the end. Write out the meanings of the suffix *-age*, and familiarize yourself with them, so that you can tell whether the short vowel-/j̆/ ending of a word is a suffix or not:

_____

_____

9. Sometimes different words formed from the same roots as words with silent letters can be helpful. In each of the following words encircle the letter which is silent in a shorter word, and underline the shorter word:

bombard	limber	signal
malignant	phlegmatic	diaphragmatic

Warning: Although the sound of the silent letter in these other forms helps you to remember it when it is silent, failure to pronounce it in still other words should not make you forget it— just because you hear no /b/ in *debtor* does not mean that there is no *b* in either *debt* or *debtor*.

10. Each of the following words contains one of the sounds we have been studying. After each word write the number of the chapter and the exercise which should have prepared you for it (5.2, for example, or 7.3):

righteous _____   exhaustion _____   tremendous _____   codger _____

Indian _____   pitcher _____   ostrich _____   virtue _____

stupendous _____   midget _____   partridge _____   rich _____

11. Supply the missing letters necessary to spell the incomplete words in the following sentences correctly:

a. He bought a sandwi_____ for his lunch.

b. He thought it a privil_____ to go to coll_____ because of the knowl_____ he would gain there.

c. They had stre_____ed the rope until it broke.

d. Your ima_____ination is too active.

e. The painting is highly ori_____inal.

f. The politician delivered his spee_____ and left immediately.

12. As a little spelling test which does not have to be dictated, we have written out in phonetic symbols the words we want you to spell. We will help you with this first one by telling you that every word here involves the question of whether or not to double one of the consonants. Write the spellings beneath the phonetic symbols:

/trip'l/	/vigər/	/prapər/	/fægət/	/æp'l/
/mægət/	/rabin/	/kapi/	/siti/	/digər/
/peb'l/	/pepər/	/rip'l/	/lepər/	/kapər/
/diti/	/papi/	/čæp'l/	/dabin/	/treb'l/

Review Lesson III: for Chapters 8-10

1. Try to formulate a generalization for final consonants (single sounds) which employ special phonograms following short vowels at the end of one-syllable words. Take into consideration /č/, /ǰ/, /f/, and /l/:

145

2. Look up the following combining forms in your dictionary and learn their meanings. They are all derived from Greek, and may help you to identify Greek roots with unusual spellings in other parts of words to which these are attached—although these are not always combined with Greek roots. As you look these up, notice the illustrations given; can you draw any conclusions as to the type of word in which a Greek root, and hence /f/ spelled *ph,* is most likely to appear? Write any such conclusions below these forms. You should try to add other Greek combining forms to this list; you will find it increasingly helpful as we go on:

grapho- (-graph)		-logy	-mania	-metry (-meter)
philo- (-phile)		-phobia	-phobe	-phone (phono-)
poly-	techno-	tele-	photo-	psych- (psycho-)

3. Underline the words in the following list which you pronounce with /ɔ/:

alkali	call	always	swat	was
dog	wrong	sloth	small	alibi
rock	loft	loss	bottle	wash

4. Answer the following questions in the space allowed:

   a. What vowel sound do you make in pronouncing a word with a silent *l* before /k/ and after an *a*?

   b. What vowel sound do you make in pronouncing a word with a silent *l* before /k/ and after an *o*?

   c. What vowel sound do you make in pronouncing a word with a silent *l* before /m/ and after an *a*?

5. The following are phonetic transcriptions of some of the commonest exceptions (other than *ph* endings) to your generalization that after a short vowel a final /f/ is spelled *ff.* Write the regular spelling underneath the phonetic transcription:

/if/	/kæf/	/rəf/	/def/	/kɔf/

/šef/	/trɔf/	/læf/	/hæf/	/klef/

6. We hope that in doing exercise 3 in Chapter 9 you discovered that only long *a* and long *i* commonly employ the vowel-consonant-silent-*e* pattern when /f/ ends a word following a long vowel. The other long vowels all use diphthongs (i.e. two vowel letters). This generalization is particularly good for one-syllable words; did you find an exception in doing exercise 3? The only common one is *waif.*

146

7. In a sense fossil blends are digraphs for the one sound which is still pronounced, and so should be considered under that sound as well as under the silent letter. As part of your review of /m/, therefore, we give below the phonetic transcriptions of some words in which it is represented by a fossil blend; under each one write the correct spelling:

/læm/   /kaHm/   /saləm/   /klaym/   /lim/

_____

/sæmən/   /saHm/   /pləmər/   /flem/   /dayəfræm/

_____

8. As part of your review now of /n/, write below the following phonetic transcriptions the correct spellings of these words:

/sayn/   /impiwn/   /niwmætik/   /məlayn/

_____

/areyn/   /nemanik/   /əlayn/   /feyn/

_____

9. Fill in the missing letters in the blanks in these sentences:

   a. The sa____on co____d swim faster than he co____d wa____k.

   b. The minister ca____mly announced the ____sa____m.

   c. The tari____ on her ta____eta dress was enou____.

   d. The do____ a____ ready looked a____ right.

   e. He sc____ded himself in the c____fee from the c____dron.

10. The modern word *sapphire* was spelled by Chaucer, writing in the fourteenth century, *saphire*. The word comes to us from the Latin word *sapphirus*. Of what linguistic phenomenon which we have already met is the modern spelling an example?

_____

Review Lesson IV: for Chapters 11-13

1. a. Make a generalization which will cover the use of *ck, tch,* and *dge:*

_____

_____

   b. What types of sounds do these digraphs and trigraphs represent?

_____

   c. Make a generalization covering the use of *ff, ss,* and *ll* at the end of one-syllable words:

_____

d. What types of sounds are /f/, /s/, and /l/?

_____

2. Answer the following questions about the symbols for /k/ which are of foreign origin:

a. Which one comes from the Greek?

_____

b. Which one comes from (primarily) Hindustani?

_____

c. Hindustani is a modern descendant of Sanskrit; read p. 130 and see if you can discover why *kh* and *k* (which represent different phonemes in Hindustani) sound alike to native speakers of English:

_____

_____

_____

d. What two phonograms come from French?

_____

e. Which one from French always comes at the end of the word?

_____

3. The following words are either real or apparent exceptions to your generalization about *ck;* look up any of which you are doubtful, and underline all real exceptions:

tic	reckon	racket	yak	sac
trek	jackal	lackey	necklace	packet
thicken	package	prickle	picket	hackney
rocket	jockey	cockpit	knuckle	cuckoo

4. In the exercises for /s/ (see 2 in Chapter 12) you made some generalizations about the spelling of /s/ at the end of a word following a consonant. Underline any exceptions:

apse	farce	response	endurance	suspense
existence	pierce	false	purse	pretense

5. In exercise 3 in Chapter 12 we asked you to make a list of words which did not agree with your generalization in exercise 1 about *ss* at the end of one-syllable words following a short vowel. How many of the following did you think of?

bus	gas	plus	pus	this	thus	us	yes

Which two of the above are or seem to be contractions of longer words or expressions?

_____

_____

6. A few verbs still allow a spelling of the past participle and past tense with *t* instead of *ed* when the latter would be pronounced /t/. At times a change in length of vowel occurs also, as in *deal* and *dealt.* Continue this list of *t*-participles, and remember that you never add *ed* to a *t* which is already an ending:

mean, meant   deal, dealt

_____

_____

_____

7. Put a circle around the silent letters in the following words:

| wrestle | coalesce | rustle | knit |
| whistle | knuckle | pestle | descent |

8. The letter *c* represents both /k/ and /s/; what are the conditions under which it represents each?

_____

_____

9. Here is another spelling test which does not need to be dictated. Beneath the phonetic transcriptions write the correct spellings:

| /kliyk/ | /keyatik/ | /iykwipt/ | /səkses/ |

_____

| /tɔk/ | /lept/ | /eyk/ | /yowk/ |

_____

Review Lesson V: for Chapters 1-13

1. List below all the abbreviations and terms for usage levels (slang, etc.) which you have encountered in your dictionary, and explain their meaning:

_____

_____

2. When your dictionary writes "Var. of . . ." after an entry, what does it mean?

_____

3. a. What two letters sound differently before *e*, *i*, and *y* from what they do before other letters?

_____

   b. How does the "division of labor" of one compare in regularity with that of the other?

_____

4. We have encountered several phonograms so far which have a definite national origin. List those which appear only in words of:

   a. Greek origin: _____

   b. French origin: _____

5. Look up the suffix *-ed* in your dictionary and then answer the following questions:

a. What meanings other than past tense does it have?

_____

b. Can you explain why *prejudice* is a common error for *prejudiced?*

_____

6. You should be able now, on the basis of what you have read, to explain why the *t* is silent in such words as *hasten, listen,* and *fasten.* Write your explanation below:

_____

_____

7. Most of the difficulty arising from the suffix *-ence* comes from deciding whether to spell it *-ance* or not, a matter which we shall take up in more detail later. But we may well digress to look at one aspect of the problem here, as it involves a review of some of the sounds we have already studied. Look at the following list of words, and below it write your explanation of the fact that there should be no doubt in any of them which spelling to use (remember that spelling is primarily the written representation of spoken sounds):

adolescence	diligence	significance
extravagance	intelligence	negligence
innocence	elegance	magnificence

_____

_____

8. Underline any words in the following list which have silent letters in your speech, and put a circle around the silent letter. These are letters you should be careful of:

government	impromptu	arctic	contemptuous
sandwich	thousandth	twelfth	length

9. Explain in turn why the silent consonant in each of the following words is silent:

a. clapboard: _____

_____

b. doubt: _____

_____

c. autumn: _____

_____

d. blackguard: _____

_____

e. succumb: _____

_____

f. handsome: _____

_____

g. science: _____

_____

h. psychology: _____

_____

i. often: _____

_____

j. knowledge: _____

_____

10. Write out the following words with the suffix *-ing* correctly added to each:

refer	change	occur	learn
appear	freshen	attach	enlarge
create	deter	lodge	patch

11. See if you can answer these questions briefly, completely, and correctly without looking back:

a. What sounds are affected by palatalization?

_____

b. What letters are influenced by this palatalization?

_____

c. What is a "syllabic"?

_____

d. What suffixes have we encountered which generally appear on roots which are no longer words in English (at least in the sense used in the word with the suffix)?

_____

e. What are the three conditions which must be met before you double the final consonant when adding a suffix beginning with a vowel?

(1) _____

_____

(2) _____

_____

(3) _____

_____

f. What is a "fossil blend"?

_____

g. When does a single consonant standing between two vowels go with the preceding vowel in syllable division?

_____

Review Lesson VI: for Chapters 14-16

1. Write in front of each of the following words the pronunciation of the letter *x* in that word, either /ks/ or /z/:

_____ express _____ annex _____ xylophone _____ axiom

_____ xenophobia _____ exit _____ reflexive _____ anxiety

2. Look up in your dictionary or in your English composition handbook the rules for forming the plurals of nouns ending in *y* and the third person singular present tense of verbs ending in *y*. Then write below each of the following words the proper plural or third person singular form:

daisy	typify	turkey	alley	allay	ally
chimney	play	study	victory	journey	try
convey	imply	trolley	employ	honey	buy

3. Get a friend to dictate this list of words to you and see how many of these /ks/ sounds you can get right the first try:

accede	exceed	accept	except	eccentric
orthodox	phonetics	oxygen	makes	hoax

4. While you have someone available, get him to dictate the following words to you, to test your memory of /i/ or /ɨ/ endings:

corbie	journey	lackey	birdie	spaghetti
petty	army	confetti	alley	loyalty

5. Here is another dictation exercise. See how many you can get right without studying them—they are all frequently misspelled. Then study them all as demons:

again   certain   bargain   villain   Britain   captain   mountain

In the final syllable of these words the digraph *ai* has been shortened until it represents /i/ or /e/ for most speakers. The commonest misspelling, however, seems not to be substituting a single vowel, but in transposing the two letters and thus creating the suffix *-ian*. Study these words ending in *-ain* carefully.

6. Underline the /ə/ sounds in the following words:

smother	drama	cucumber	conundrum
oven	enough	dungeon	wholesome

7. In exercise 1a. in Chapter 15 we asked you to think of one-syllable words ending in /z/ following a short vowel, putting those which used *zz* for /z/ in one column of the wordlists, and those which used other phonograms in another. Some of the words involved are so common that we suspect you did not think of them, and so below we give a list of the commonest words which do *not* use *zz*. How many of them did you have in your list? Does this list alter in any way your answer to questions e. and f. in this same exercise in Chapter 15?

as	has	says	fez	his
is	quiz	whiz	was	does

---

8. Here is a quick quiz. Answer the following questions briefly and quickly. Do not verify any of your answers until you have completed the entire quiz. Then look back to see how accurate you have been:

a. What phonograms can represent /z/ at the beginning of a word?

b. In the middle of a word?

c. Before /m/?

d. Jot down quickly all the words you can remember which end in *zz*:

e. What phonograms can represent /ks/ at the beginning of a word?

f. In the middle of a word?

g. At the end when not including inflectional *-s*?

h. What phonograms can represent /i/ at the end of a word?

i. Elsewhere in a word?

j. What phonograms can represent /ə/ at the beginning of a word?

_____

k. At the end of a word?

_____

Exceptional phonograms, occurring in only one or perhaps two demons, are not to be included in the above answers.

Review Lesson VII: for Chapters 17-19

1. Below are some of the commonest Latin roots providing nouns ending in *-sion*. A large proportion of these nouns come from these few verbs. We have given you the Latin word and the form in which it appears in English; *you* provide the illustrative English nouns ending in *-sion,* filling in the blank spaces at the right:

Latin	English form	
cedere, cessus	cede, ceed, cess	_____
cutere, cussus	cuss	_____
fateri, fessus	fess	_____
gradi, gressus	grade, gress	_____
merger, mersus	merge, mers(e)	_____
mittere, missus	mit, miss	_____
pandere, pansus	pand, pans(e)	_____
pellere, pulsus	pel, puls(e)	_____
pendere, pensus	pend, pens(e)	_____
prehendere, prehensus	prehend, prehens(e)	_____
premere, pressus	press	_____
scendere, scensus (a late form of scandere)	scend, scens(e), scent	_____
possidere, possessus	possess	_____
tendere, tensus	tend, tens(e), tent	_____
vertere, versus	vert, vers(e)	_____

You should familiarize yourself, through your dictionary, with the meanings of these Latin roots to avoid any confusion.

2. Words are like human beings, they like to follow the crowd, or, as philologists express it, act by analogy. You may see a nice example of linguistic analogy if you look up the derivations of *connection* and *complexion*. There is just as much logic for the *-xion* ending in one as in the other. But

there are so many words spelled -*ction* that *connection* has been drawn to that spelling. *Complexion*, not being used so frequently, has not felt this attraction so strongly. Can you discover any other words which, like *connection*, have been drawn from the -*xion* ending to the -*ction* ending?

_____

_____

3. If you are still uncertain about the sound we represent by /ər/, try pronouncing the following pairs of words, in which the common syllable with /r/ is usually pronounced differently in the two words—the right-hand one being /ər/:

error	erring	kerosene	kernel
interfere	infer	ire	irk
clerical	clergy	capture	captor

4. The phonogram *ar* for the troublesome /ər/ appears most of the time in final syllables—another reason perhaps why *separate* has become such a demon. Most of the time this final syllable is unaccented and a suffix. As a little practice in identifying suffixes when you meet them, look at the following words in which *ar* represents /ər/, underline the words with a suffix and encircle those whose ending is not a suffix:

hazard	pedlar	dollar	hangar	backward
liar	grammar	westward	angular	standard

5. The commonest spelling for /ər/ is *er*. The answers to the following questions may help to guide you in selecting it at the proper moments:

   a. What common words begin with /ər/ spelled *er*?

_____

   b. What common suffixes are spelled -*er*?

_____

   c. What is the proportion of words beginning with *per-* to those beginning with *pur-*?

_____

   d. What spelling is most common for /ər/ in medial syllables?

_____

6. Unlike *ar*, which usually appears in unaccented syllables, *ir* usually appears in accented ones. The answers to the following questions may help to guide you in your choice:

   a. Is the assimilated prefix *ir-* ever pronounced /ər/?

_____

   b. Familiarize yourself with the prefix *circum-;* how is it pronounced and what does it mean?

_____

   c. What words begin with /ər/ spelled *ir*?

_____

   d. This phonogram appears at the end of a multisyllabic word only rarely, and as these are somewhat unusual words, we shall list the most common ones for you here: *elixir, nadir, tapir,* and *triumvir*—examples also of *ir* appearing in unaccented syllables, which is unusual. Familiarize yourself with these words, and add them to your vocabulary.

   e. The phonogram *ir* is most common in one-syllable words. The following rhyming families will help you; see how many eye-rhymes as well as ear-rhymes you can add to each column:

bird	girl	firm	dirt	stir

   f. It frequently appears also in the first, accented syllable of longer words, such as *circle.* List below as many other examples as you can, excluding words beginning with *circum-:*

7. The phonogram *or* provides us with a nice illustration of the fact that the sounds of a word influence one another. In the main part of the word, *or* is pronounced /ər/ only when it follows /w/, as in *work* and *word.* The rest of the time it appears at the end of the word, most frequently as a suffix. Just because there is a /w/ before /ər/ does not mean that the spelling will be *or,* of course, but the absence of the /w/ will eliminate one phonogram from your consideration. The answers to the following questions should help you with *or* at the end of a word:

   a. What is the difference between the suffixes *-er* and *-or* when they are similar in meaning? (Look them both up in your dictionary. A knowledge of French or Latin will help you.)

   b. What is the meaning of the verb suffix *-ate?*

   c. How do verbs in *-ate* (there are over 300 of them) form their agent nouns, or words for the person or thing which does what the root says?

   d. You might find it useful to review the list of words which you began on page 90 of words ending in *-or* when these letters are not a suffix.

8. The phonogram *ur* is the second most common to represent /ər/, and the one most difficult to distinguish from *er.* For one thing, there are a good many homonyms to keep straight, such as *serge* and *surge, serf* and *surf.* The answers to the following may prove helpful:

   a. What common words begin with *ur* representing /ər/?

   b. What is the proportion of words beginning with *sur-* to those beginning with *ser-?*

156

c. A number of very common roots contain this phonogram also, such as *-cur* (Latin) and *turn* (Old English). How many others can you add which appear in at least half a dozen words?

_____

9. The other three phonograms for /ər/ provide only a few examples each. The answers to the following exercises should provide you with some help:

a. How many words can you write down here which are eye-rhymes as well as ear-rhymes of the following:

　　　　earl　　　　　　　　　earn　　　　　　　　　earth

_____

_____

_____

b. If you wrote down one or two words under each of the above words, you now have in front of you words which, with their compounds and derivatives, make up about half the words in which *ear* is pronounced /ər/. Can you add any other words below?

_____

_____

c. Other than the nouns ending in *-or* which the British prefer to spell *-our* (*honour, colour,* and *valour,* for example), there are only a handful of words with the phonogram *-our* for /ər/. Half of them contain the root *journ* as in *journey.* Write down below as many other examples of the use of this root in English as you can think of (don't look under *j* in your dictionary):

_____

_____

_____

d. The phonogram *yr* appears in only five words that are at all common. It is rather difficult to be inductive about so small a group of words, so you might do well to learn them individually as demons:

　martyr　　　　　myrrh　　　　　myrtle　　　　　satyr　　　　　zephyr

What is the national origin of these words?

_____

10. See how quickly you can answer these questions without looking back; then look back and check your answers:

a. After what letters may you use *-tion?*

_____

b. After what letters may you use *-sion?*

_____

c. What is the national origin of *rh* for /r/?

_____

d. Spell two words beginning with *rh* commonly associated with poetry (and used as illustrations in our word lists):

_____

e. What two words represent /u/ with *o*?

_____

f. What is the national origin of *ea* as a spelling for /e/?

_____

g. What is the national origin of *ou* as a spelling for /u/?

_____

11. It is important in using suffixes to remember what it is that you are adding to, and that a word may have more than one suffix. The student who writes *critism (a common error) for *criticism* has added -*ism* on to the wrong word-element. Beside each of the following suffixes write the part of speech *to which* it is commonly added:

-ism _____ -ish _____ -able _____ -est _____ -ful _____

-less _____ -ly (2) _____ -hood _____ -ment _____ -ness _____

12. Write out the adjective forms ending in -*al* that are companion words to the following: (watch your step!)

existence _____ space _____ finance _____ society _____

circumstance _____ palace _____ glacier _____ face _____

13. What is the meaning of the suffix -*ive*, and how is it pronounced? Write out your answer below, with a few words illustrative of this very useful suffix:

_____

_____

14. One of the most troublesome groups of words using *ea* to represent /e/ are the verbs in which the past tense has shortened the vowel without changing the spelling, as in *mean* and *meant*, or the two tenses of *read*. Add any others that you can think of here:

_____

_____

_____

_____

Review Lesson VIII: for Chapters 20-23

1. Can you answer these questions about silent letters without looking back?

   a. When is *w* most commonly silent in the middle of a word?

   _____

   b. When is *w* most likely to be silent at the beginning of a word?

   _____

   c. Under what circumstances is *h* most likely to be silent in the middle of a word?

   _____

2. Answer the following questions about *x* without looking back:

   a. When does *x* represent /gz/?

   _____

   b. When does *x* represent /gž/?

   _____

   c. When does *x* represent /kš/?

   _____

3. Here is another quick quiz to do as rapidly as possible:

   a. What letter represents /ŋ/ besides *ng,* and when?

   _____

   b. What phonogram which we have just taken up represents two sounds? _____

   What are they? _____
   c. How many sounds or combinations of sounds can *x* represent?

   _____

   d. What sounds are represented in reverse in modern spelling?

   _____

   e. What combination of sounds does *gn* represent?

   _____

   f. Does *gn* always represent this combination?

   _____

   g. How is /kw/ usually represented in English?

   _____

4. In the following words encircle every *w* which you pronounce:

sword	two	wrought	whoop	swoop	whom
whole	wrench	whopping	whore	swore	answer

5. Before the following words write the phonetic symbols for the sounds represented by the *gn* or *ng* combinations of letters:

_____ flinger   _____ astringent   _____ lorgnette   _____ arrangement

_____ tangible   _____ stronger   _____ recognize   _____ cognac

6. Here is another spelling test requiring no dictation. Beneath each phonetic transcription write the correct spelling of the word represented:

/egzistəns/   /hweθər/   /liŋgər/   /viynyet/   /riyð/

_____

/viyəment/   /briyθ/   /aŋkšəs/   /huw/   /estreynǰ/

_____

Review Lesson IX: for Chapters 14-23

1. When an independent word like *full* is used as a suffix, the combining form is sometimes not spelled the same way as the independent word, as is true of *-ful*. What generalization, which we took up some time ago, applies here?

_____

_____

2. In making a list of words ending in a short vowel followed by *ve*, did you discover anything interesting about the spelling of /ə/ before /v/? You should have; write it here:

_____

_____

3. Look up in your dictionary all the words beginning with *swo-* and *who-*, to see how well they seem to follow the generalization that *w* is silent when following a consonant and preceding /uw/ or long *o*. Write down what you find out:

_____

_____

4. Without looking back, see if you can arrange below in different categories or groups all the possible ways of representing /ks/ which appear at all commonly in English:

_____

_____

5. One general observation of students' spelling would be that a common source of trouble not covered by any rules is the student's failure to include all the letters when a word ends in the same sound as or a sound similar to the first sound of the suffix—for example, *study, studying; sudden, suddenness; govern, government.* In the following exercises we are going to give you some practice in adding suffixes, with this type of word in every exercise:

a. Write the past participle (i.e. the form ending in *-ed*) below each of the following verbs:

annul	free	plan	stop	tie

bivouac	outrage	rent	control	transfer

travel	hoe	notice	dry	ally

b. Add *-ing* to the following verbs:

tax	come	die	quarrel	modify

hope	send	toe	refer	taxi

study	shine	write	ski	lie

c. Add *-ment* to the following words:

abridge	merry	develop	judge	entangle

govern	prefer	install	comply	state

d. Add *-ness* to the following words:

sudden	dull	busy	open	coy

shy	drunken	direct	thin	dry

e. Add *-ly* to the following words:

immediate	accidental	usual	happy	casual

real	wry	gay	dull	open

f. Add *-ous* to the following words:

riot	joy	desire	poison	courage

pity	duty	plenty	bounty	beauty

avarice	grace	vice	space	caprice

The last two rows above constitute two rather special groups; formulate generalizations for them below:

_____

_____

g. Add *-able* to the following words:

read	move	play	ply	change

prefer	comfort	control	conquer	desire

h. What happens to the words you have just written (and those ending in *-ible*) when you add *-ly* to them? Write out the ten words above with both *-able* and *-ly* added to them, and formulate a generalization as to what happens:

_____

_____

_____

6. Add *-sion* or *-tion*, whichever is correct, onto the roots of the following words; write the resulting word, properly spelled, beneath the original word:

divide	collect	discrete	confuse	assert

extend	divert	permit	attend	exempt

7. Here is another quick quiz. Do these exercises as rapidly as you can without looking back until you have tried them all; then check your answers, which you should write in after each question:

a. What is the commonest spelling for /z/?

_____

b. How is /ə/ commonly spelled at the end of a word?

_____

162

c. What suffixes have a /ə/ sound in them?

_____

d. What prefixes have a /ə/ sound in them?

_____

e. Which prefixes most commonly assimilate?

_____

f. What is the national origin of words using *rh* for /r/?

_____

g. How do you form the plurals of words ending in *-ey*?

_____

h. What sounds may be represented by *qu*?

_____

i. What is the commonest phonogram to represent /ər/?

_____

j. Where does it most frequently appear?

_____

8. Whether one selects the ending *-sion* or *-tion*, *-ance* or *-ence,* depends upon the conjugation to which the Latin root originally belonged—a fact which may at first glance seem to be of little help to those who have studied no Latin. But if you know that *incursion* is spelled with *-sion* (as you should from the pronunciation, /žən/ being always spelled *-sion*), then you can know that *occurrence* is spelled with *-ence,* because normally *-sion* and *-ence* are added to the same roots, and *-tion* and *-ance* to others. There are, of course, exceptions, such as *admission* and *admittance,* but if you are uncertain and have to guess, at least make it an educated guess—the percentages will be in your favor! Look back at the list of Latin verbs in Review Lesson VII, page 154, for which you have provided examples of nouns ending in *-sion.* Below write examples of nouns ending in *-ence,* at least one for each of the Latin verbs given:

_____

_____

_____

_____

_____

_____

_____

Review Lesson X: for Chapters 24-26

1. Give illustrative words below to show what phonograms are most commonly used to represent long *o*, long *i*, and long *e* respectively at the end of words:

_____

_____

_____

2. Give below illustrations of the commonest representation of these three long vowels in words of one syllable ending in a consonant:

_____

_____

3. Do the same for the commonest representation of these long vowels in final syllables of multi-syllabic words where a consonant ends this syllable:

_____

_____

4. How are these long vowels represented in syllables ending in a consonant and not final syllables, other than compound words?

_____

_____

5. From answering these first four questions, have you any observations to make as to the relative consistency with which these vowels follow the ideal pattern we discussed back on pages 11–12 and again on page 102?

_____

_____

6. From answering all these questions, can you make any observations about the length of the roots which you encountered in multisyllabic words? Were they two- and three-syllable roots, or only one-syllable words and roots with prefixes and suffixes added?

_____

_____

_____

7. List all the words you can think of which have *ei* representing a *short* vowel. We have already mentioned one in which it represents /e/ and three in which it represents /i/, but you will find that some of the words we have discussed under long *e* have equally acceptable pronunciations with short vowels for the *ei*. Look up the four words we have already listed, and write them in below, along with any others in which you pronounce the *ei* as a short vowel:

_____

_____

8. In a previous exercise we asked you to list all the words that rhymed with *four*. What other words can you write below in which long *o* is represented by *ou*? Include words using *-ough* too:

_____

_____

9. Write below the following words as many others as you can which rhyme with them and have the French *i* for long *e*. What conclusion can you draw as to what letter appears most commonly after it?

machine   critique   valise   police

_____

_____

10. Add as many eye- and ear-rhymes to the two lists below as you can, and then answer the questions:

nigh   light

_____

_____

_____

_____

    a. Can you think of any other words, other than compounds and derivatives of these words, that use *-igh* as a phonogram for long *i*? If so, list them here:

_____

_____

_____

_____

    b. Look up the suffixes *-en;* which one is used in the word *lighten*?

_____

    c. What is the difference between *lightening* and *lightning*? (You may find the etymology of *lightning* helpful. These two words are frequently confused.)

_____

_____

11. This is another dictationless spelling test; write the correct spelling beneath the phonetic transcription:

/blaynd/	/kəmbaynd/	/kowld/	/θow/	/rowld/

/debriy/	/ələmniy/	/refəriy/	/riysiyt/	/kənfowrm/

/fatiyg/	/laytniŋ/	/biyhaynd/	/ǰowlt/	/suwpərsiyd/

/wiyld/	/metafowr/	/fowrd/	/sayk'l/	/liyžuwr/

Review Lesson XI: for Chapters 27-29

1. Because /uw/ and long *u* or /iw/ are so easily confused, it is important to know when to distinguish between them. Answer the following questions for *both* sounds; if the answer is the same for both, you need write it only once:

a. What phonogram(s) do you commonly use at the end of syllables other than final syllables?

b. What phonogram(s) do you use most commonly at the end of words?

c. What phonogram(s) did you find of distinctive national origin, and for what sound(s)?

d. What phonogram(s) do you most commonly use in syllables ending in a consonant at the end of a word?

e. In answering question d., could you see any distinction made between one-syllable words and longer ones?

f. What phonogram(s) do you use in syllables ending in a consonant, other than a final syllable?

g. What phonogram(s) are limited to only one of the two sounds, and which one?

/uw/:   /iw/:

h. After what sounds will you almost always hear /uw/, and after what sounds, /iw/?

/uw/:   /iw/:

_____

_____

2. We turn now to a different style of questioning about /uw/ and /iw/. The following questions deal more with the phonogram itself:

   a. Where does *u* usually appear?

_____

   b. Where else does it occasionally appear?

_____

   c. Where do you almost invariably use *ue*?

_____

   d. Where is *ew* most commonly used?

_____

   e. In what other positions may it appear?

      for both sounds? _____

_____

      how commonly? _____

_____

   f. The combination *u*-consonant-silent-*e* appears most commonly where?

_____

   g. Is it preferred in one-syllable words or longer ones or is no preference shown?

_____

   h. Where can you use *oo*?

_____

   i. What does your last answer suggest as to how to study words with *oo*?

_____

   j. The importance of the preceding consonant sound in dealing with /uw/ and /iw/ may be seen by what is happening to *ou* (normally always pronounced /uw/) and to *eu* (normally always sounded /iw/). Look up the pronunciations of *coupon* and of *rheum* and its derivatives. What do you find?

_____

_____

3. This seems like a good time to review some of the generalizations involving /iw/ which we learned some time ago. Write in your answer to these questions below:

   a. What is the spelling of /z/ after /iw/? See exercise 4a. in Chapter 15 (page 70).

   _____

   b. What sometimes happens to /s/ before /iw/? See exercises 2d. and 2e. in Chapter 17 (pages 83–4).

   _____

   c. What sometimes happens to /t/ before /iw/? See exercise 5 in Chapter 5 (page 40).

   _____

   d. What sometimes happens to /d/ before /iw/? See exercise 5 in Chapter 6 (page 43).

   _____

   e. When the sound of the consonant preceding /iw/ changes, the new sound determines how much of the /i/-element is left in the /iw/—that is, whether it is still /iw/ or instead, /uw/. When you think you are dealing with an example of palatalization, the process of elimination will help your spelling; what phonograms can you immediately dismiss as possibilities in spelling these words?

   _____

4. Below are some words which have homonyms involving one of the vowels which we have studied this week. Below each one write the word with which it is easily confused, making sure that you know the meaning of both words in each pair:

break	fair	plain	rain (2)	new
troop	great	vain (2)	rood	hew
you're	whose	threw	chute	dew (2)

5. Here are a few demons which we omitted earlier, but which you can work on now. Look up pronunciations, derivations, and meanings of all of them:

   adieu   beauty   brougham   debut   lieu   through   tulle

6. Answer the following questions about /ey/:

   a. What is the commonest spelling of /ey/ at the end of a word?

   _____

   b. Can you make a generalization about the symbol for /ey/ when it is followed by a consonant in a one-syllable word?

   _____

c. Can you make a generalization about the symbol for /ey/ when it is followed by *two* consonant sounds in a one-syllable word?

_____

_____

d. The only exceptions to the generalization which you should have just made are, in addition to past tenses and participles which have /d/ or /t/, two rhyming families. How many words can you add to these two examples?

          waste   change

_____

_____

_____

_____

e. What is the commonest spelling of /ey/ followed by a consonant in final syllables of multisyllabic words?

_____

f. What is the commonest spelling of /ey/ followed by a consonant in other than final syllables?

_____

g. What is the usual spelling for /ey/ at the end of other than final syllables?

_____

h. From answering the above, what do you think the most satisfactory way is to study the words with the phonograms *ea, ei, eigh,* or *ey* for /ey/?

_____

_____

i. What *short* vowels have we found *ai* representing? Look back at pages 50, 91 and 152 for some examples, and make a generalization about them here:

_____

_____

Review Lesson XII: for Chapters 30-32

1. The following questions about the special nuclei are designed to help you generalize about them as a group, and see what is distinctive about each:

a. What is the usual spelling for each at the end of a word?

_____

b. What is the usual spelling for each before a vowel?

_____

c. What is the usual spelling for each before a consonant?

_____

d. Which one of the three follows the ideal pattern for these special nuclei most faithfully?

_____

e. What special phonogram represents /aw/ in a few words?

_____

f. What complications make /oH/ difficult?

_____

g. What irregularities occur with /oy/?

_____

h. Are there many words other than compound words or derivatives which have more than one syllable and employ a special nucleus in other than a final syllable?

_____

2. The following demons represent the only common examples of the use of a particular phonogram for the nucleus it represents. Use your special method of study for demons if they cause you trouble:

sauerkraut	broad	buoy

3. /oH/ at the end of a word does not seem to be represented by either *-augh* or *-ough,* but otherwise do these phonograms seem to follow the pattern of *-igh* for /ay/, *-eigh* for /ey/, and *-ough* for /aw/ and /ow/?   Describe the pattern here:

_____

_____

4. Here is another non-dictated spelling test, which includes some very easy words and some demons. As before, write the correct spelling below the phonetic transcription:

/broHd/	/rayl/	/plaw/	/flaw'r/
/klawd/	/doHtər/	/ðoHt/	/θaw/
/boykat/	/grawl/	/æploHz/	/ǰoynt/

170

Review Lesson XIII: for Chapters 24-32

1. Except in compounds and derivatives, what phonogram is most likely to represent a long vowel in the early syllables of a multisyllabic word, regardless of which long vowel you are speaking?

_____

2. The phonogram *ue,* as we have seen, may represent either /uw/ or /iw/, usually at the end of a word. In addition to this confusion, it sometimes (but not always) drops the *e* before adding a suffix beginning with a consonant. Look up the correct spellings for the following combinations, and write them in below:

   argue   ment   true   ly   due   ly

_____

3. The combining form of *all* is *al,* and it may appear at the beginning or the end of a word, as in *already* and *withal.* Some of the most troublesome homonyms or near-homonyms are created by the fact that the words which combine with *all* are also used with them in an uncombined manner. Below you have the uncombined forms; write in the combined forms, and the meanings of both:

   all mighty   all most   all one   all ready   all so   all though   all together   all ways

_____

Some of these pairs will be much less troublesome than others because the two words are rarely used together except in their combined form. *All* is frequently used, however, with certain other words with which it never combines, such as *around* (and *round*), *clear, fours, right, told,* and *wrong.* Do not make a mistake by combining any of these words with *all* into one word.

4. For many people the *a* in *wharf* and *quarter* represents an /oH/ sound. In adding these words to the wordlists in our last lesson, in which column would you put them? Justify your decision below:

_____

_____

_____

5. Here is another quick quiz; answer these as rapidly as possible without looking back. When you have finished, check your answers:

   a. What sounds have we now met which may be represented by *ow?* Give an illustrative word for each:

_____

   b. What sounds may be represented by *ou?* Again, give an illustrative word for each:

_____

   c. What sounds may be represented by *ei?* (One of them we have not mentioned in the last nine chapters.) Give an illustrative word for each:

_____

d. What sounds may be represented by *ea*? (Again, one of your answers is in a lesson earlier than one of the last nine chapters.) Give illustrative words:

_____

e. What sounds may be represented by *ie*? (One of your answers is ancient history again.) Give illustrative words:

_____

_____

_____

f. Outline here the basic four-phonogram pattern of the long vowels:

_____

_____

_____

_____

_____

g. In what general ways do the long vowels vary this pattern?

_____

_____

h. Outline here the basic two-phonogram pattern of the so-called special nuclei which we have been discussing:

_____

_____

_____

_____

i. In what ways in general do these vowels vary this pattern?

_____

_____

j. List below the phonograms of foreign origin which we have found for the long vowels. Put an asterisk beside those which are used for other sounds as well, to remind you to be especially careful with them:

_____

_____

_____

Review Lesson XIV: for Chapters 1-33

1. Here is a quick review of suffixes:

   a. Add *-ly* to the following words:

universal	true	probable	credible	due

general	whole	capable	careful	indispensable

   b. Add *-ment* to the following words:

govern	argue	develop	judge

comply	install	abridge	merry

   c. Add *-ing* to the following words:

study	lie	ski	write	tax	die

modify	taxi	toe	send	refer	total

   d. Add *-ed* to the following words:

free	plan	annul	tie	panic	travel

occur	dry	stop	control	plane	cure

   e. Add *-ness* to the following words:

busy	shy	coy	dull	open	drunken

   f. Add *-ous* to the following words:

desire	vice	plenty	joy	riot	courage

g. Add *-able* to the following words:

change	ply	move	read	play	like

dance	size	peace	regret	decoy	perish

h. What happens to *full* and *all* when these words become combining forms and are used as suffixes?

2. Here is a quick review of prefixes:
   a. Add the negative prefix *in-* to the following words:

logical	organic	religious	possible

capable	mature	proper	legal

b. To the following Latin roots add the Latin prefix *ad-;* write the resulting English word below the Latin root:

-test	-stringe	-sperse	-sent	-nul

-scend	-rive	-quaint	-leviate	-opt

-pear	-bridge	-cede	-fect	-gravate

c. To the following Latin roots add the Latin prefix *com-;* write the resulting English word below the Latin root:

-bine	-pose	-mit	-dole	-fer

-cise	-lect	-rode	-cur	-here

d. To the following Latin roots add the Latin prefix *en-;* write the resulting English word below the Latin root:

-bellish	-phasis	-piric	-large	-dow

174

e. To the following Latin roots add the Latin prefix *ex-;* write the resulting English word below the Latin root:

-change -cite -port -fort -dict -vict

f. To the following Latin roots add the Latin prefix *ob-;* write the resulting English word below the Latin root:

-ject -tuse -casion -fer -press -durate

g. To the following Latin roots add the Latin prefix *sub-;* write the resulting English word below the Latin root:

-ject -sist -vert -fice -gest -ply

h. Combine *all* as a prefix with as many of the following words as possible, writing the correct spelling of the new word below the old one:

ready one right together ways

wrong most though mighty wet

3. What are the phenomena which cause 90 per cent of the double letters in the English language?

4. What phenomena tend to create a special phonogram for a sound?

Illustrate:

5. Put a circle around any of the following consonant sequences which would not appear in English, and be prepared to explain orally why it would not occur:

tch dg ngk cks zm gzh cw ks hw shs

6. The following phonograms will generally be found in only one or two positions in a word (except for compounds and derivatives, of course). Indicate under each one where you are most likely to find it:

tch	ough	eigh	j	ow
ff	oy	dge	v	ue
ie	ti	ee	ll	ay

7. Cite as many examples as you can (a minimum of two) of *types* of situation in which the presence of a vowel or a consonant before a sound may alter its spelling:

_____

_____

_____

_____

8. What three conditions must a word meet to double its final consonant before a suffix beginning with a vowel?

(1) _____

(2) _____

(3) _____

9. When do you change *y* to *i* in adding a suffix to a word?

_____

10. When do you drop the silent *e* in adding a suffix to a word?

_____

11. Describe in your own words the basic pattern for long vowels, and comment on how well each long vowel adheres to that pattern:

_____

_____

_____

12. Describe the basic pattern for the so-called special nuclei, and comment on how well each one adheres to that pattern:

_____

_____

_____

_____

176

13. Could you see any pattern for the short vowels? Describe as much as you could discover:

_____

_____

14. How much pattern did you find for the consonants? Describe what you saw here:

_____

_____

15. At the end of Chapter 4 we asked you to accept our word for four generalizations, based on generalizations which you have since made. Look back at Chapter 4 (pages 36–7), and see if you can list here some of the generalizations which support each of the four made there:

_____

_____

_____

_____

Review Lesson XV: for Chapters 1-33

Mnemonic Devices

Mnemonic devices, or tricks to help the memory remember the spelling of an individual word, are in general extravagant of time and effort for what one learns. The same amount of time spent in learning a generalization or a rhyming family of exceptions would add a group of words to your list of known words and be much more economical of effort. There are times, however, when generalizations and rhyming families fail to help, and a demon seems to defy the best methods of study. On these occasions mnemonic devices may be a real help, just as when one has a broken leg, one needs a crutch. Remember that as soon as the leg is well (the word is learned), the crutch (the mnemonic device) should be discarded.

The best mnemonic devices are probably those which you think up for yourself and which have some direct connection with the spelling rather than a distortion of the pronunciation. One which I used successfully as a college student was for *separate*. The word kept tripping me up in themes and exams, and in my opinion was "a rat." To my delight I discovered one day that the word itself admitted the truth of my feelings—you can see it in the spelling: *sepARATe*. (I have noticed since that others have made this same discovery.)

A few more examples may help you to make your own mnemonic devices. The word *indispensable* has caused much trouble. One student remembered that it began like *India*, but you had to wait for the end of the word to find the *a*. Another remembered that "sable (i.e. the fur) is indispensable to many women." Actually this word ought not to cause so much trouble, because there is a good generalization to cover the trouble spot. In most cases you will add -able on to roots which are words in English (minus the silent e, of course, when there is one), as in *dependable, believable, dispensable;* you will add -ible on to roots which are not words in English, as *credible, feasible. Indispensable* is, after all, only the perfectly regular *dispensable* with the negative prefix *in-* added.

Another troublesome word is *cemetery.* Remember, as one college professor is reported to have told his class, "We get there with e's." *Corps,* another demon because of its silent letters, should not be killed by adding an e to it. And finally, *develop* may be spelled with a final silent e, but for the preferred spelling you "lop off the e."

No mnemonic device can be successful which does not cope with the particular part of the word which is bothering you. The ability to see where your difficulty lies, to see the trouble spot in a word, is important, and we shall give you some practice at it. A word may have more than one trouble spot, or it may be the entire word, as when you confuse homonyms. Oftentimes merely taking the time to analyze what your mistake has been is needed, and the mnemonic device is unnecessary. But be sure your analysis is correct. I have seen students, asked to correct their papers, substitute one misspelling for another simply because they were too hurried or lazy to check their correction with the dictionary.

Learning to spell, as Thorstein Veblen once said, takes time, but if you are going to be in a profession or position where you will be judged by your spelling, it will be time well spent. You should, however, be learning how to spend your time effectively, and we seriously question whether learning mnemonic devices warrants the time spent on it.

Below is a list of commonly misspelled words, taken from over 2000 freshman themes, totalling over 1,500,000 words, written at Trinity College. If you would like to compare this with a very similar one from a large mid-western university, you may do so by looking at the list in Easley S. Jones's *Practical Composition.* The differences between the two lists are to be expected from differences in theme topics assigned; the interesting fact is that there are so many similarities. As we said earlier, the ability to see what causes the trouble in a word is important—it puts you on your guard. We want you to practice this analysis here: we have shown you how with the first fifteen words on the list; you write in analyses of all the others. The first fifty words are arranged in the order of the frequency of their misspelling; the second fifty are arranged alphabetically:

    its (you have to distinguish between a pronoun and a contraction)
    too (you must learn the difference between homonyms, one of which is an adverb, and one a preposition)
    appropriate (do not start the third syllable before you finish the second)
    prejudiced (how do you make an adjective from a noun or a verb?)
5 immigrant (you must distinguish this from a near-homonym)

    Negroes (look up how to form the plural of nouns ending in *o*)
    lose (you have to distinguish two near-homonyms)
    sentence (get the suffix correct)
    precede (what verbs, now, end in -*ceed?*)
10 almost (what is the combining form of *all?* What does *most* mean?)

    conscious (this is a demon, with *sc* for /s/. Remember it)
    appear (do you recognize the assimilation? Then double the *p*)
    married (the double letter here is not so easy to remember, but try)
    conversation (don't leave out a syllable; *conversion* may result from *conversation,* but they are not the same)
15 an (there are two indefinite articles; where do you use which?)

    separate
    siege
    prove
    against
20 to

title
their
effect
definite
25 existence

grammar
judgment
led
occurred
30 suppress

proceed
repetition
interest
versatile
35 signal

engines
councilor
antiseptic
sleeve
40 description

equipment
here
occasion
possess
45 similar

affect
disapprove
basically
independence
50 quantity

already
always
amateur
argument
55 calculate

chose (and chosen)
conceive
connoisseur
control
60 criticize

crowd
degree
derelict
discoveries
65 dissection

embarrass
environment
except
familiar
70 fascinating

flourish
forward
frightening
gardener
75 hurriedly

imbecile
immediately
inevitably
influential
80 initiate

irrelevant
it's
knowledge
marriage
85 meant

noticeable
optimist
populace
prepare
90 procedure

receive
resemblance
roommate
schedule
95 statement

stretch
surprise
than
weird
100 whereabouts

There is an old saying among electrical appliance salesmen that if one of their products fails to perform properly, it is never the fault of the machine but that of the person who tried to operate it. After inspecting the above list of words, would you agree that this saying could be paraphrased to say that whenever there is an undue amount of misspelling, the fault lies not with the language but with the speller?